SCIENCE FICTION

This is a volume in the
Arno Press collection

SCIENCE FICTION

ADVISORY EDITORS

R. Reginald

Douglas Menville

See last pages of this volume
for a complete list of titles

A HISTORICAL AND CRITICAL SURVEY OF THE SCIENCE-FICTION FILM

Douglas Menville

ARNO PRESS

A New York Times Company

New York — 1975

Reprint Edition 1974 by Arno Press Inc.

SCIENCE FICTION
ISBN for complete set: 0-405-06270-2
See last pages of this volume for titles.

Manufactured in the United States of America

Library of Congress Cataloging in Publication Data

Menville, Douglas Alver.
A historical and critical survey of the science fiction film.

(Science fiction)
Originally presented as the author's thesis (M. A.), University of Southern California, 1959.
Bibliography: p.
1. Science fiction films--History and criticism.
I. Title. II. Series.
PN1995.9.S26M4 791.43'0909'15 74-16509
ISBN 0-405-06330-X

A HISTORICAL AND CRITICAL SURVEY OF THE SCIENCE-FICTION FILM

by

Douglas Menville

A Thesis Presented to the

FACULTY OF THE GRADUATE SCHOOL

UNIVERSITY OF SOUTHERN CALIFORNIA

In Partial Fulfillment of the

Requirements for the Degree

Master of Arts

(Cinema)

June 1959

To my Mother and Father,
with love,
this small return
on a large investment,

and to
Mike Burgess,
a true friend,
who made it happen.

"Two things fill the mind with ever new and increasing wonder and awe—the starry heavens above me and the moral law within me."

—Kant, *Critique of Pure Reason*, Conclusion

TABLE OF CONTENTS

ACKNOWLEDGMENTS

Since the rigors of thesis format do not allow for an acknowledgments page, I have had to wait over a decade to express these. They are no less heartfelt today than they were in 1959.

I am deeply grateful to the following people for their assistance and encouragement on this project: Dr. Richard Dyer MacCann, who bravely championed my cause with the thesis committee and convinced them to let me tackle the subject of science-fiction films, and whose friendship and encouragement meant a great deal to me when I most needed it; Maynard T. Smith, without whose efforts in supervising the typing and untying red tape this thesis would never have made its deadline; the late Henry Kuttner, one of our finest science-fiction writers, who was kind enough to share his ideas and opinions on the science-fiction film with me shortly before his death; Ray Bradbury, George Pal and Forrest J Ackerman, who graciously took the time to read this thesis and offer helpful comments on it; my co-editor on this series, Robert Reginald, a good friend who has made a ten-year dream become a reality; and our lovely editor at Arno, Sherry Olynyk, whose labors in my behalf on this project are greatly appreciated.

INTRODUCTION

At the time this thesis was written, in 1959, the science-fiction film was not taken very seriously in academic or critical circles, and for good reason. If you looked at the current crop of poorly-made, low-budget "gigantic creature" films then glutting the theaters (see pp. 141-142 for a partial listing), you would find very little that could be considered serious cinematic art. These science-fiction horror films were giving the entire *genre* a bad name.

Having had a lifelong love affair with science fiction in general and the science-fiction film in particular, and seeing that no serious book-length treatment of the latter was available, I felt the time had come to attempt one. My reasons for writing such a study were threefold: first, to provide a reference work where none existed before for those students and researchers like myself interested in the science-fiction film; second, to demonstrate, by means of a comprehensive critical history of the field, that science-fiction films have been, and could be again, a serious and relevant type of motion picture, offering food for thought as well as good entertainment; and third, to complete my requirements for a degree of Master of Arts in the Cinema Department of the University of Southern California with a thesis on a subject of great interest to me.

As you might imagine, I encountered some difficulty in convincing my thesis committee that such a subject could be handled with proper academic dignity, but thanks largely to the efforts of Dr. Richard Dyer MacCann, then an instructor in the Cinema Department, who believed in me, if not in the *genre* itself, I was allowed to proceed. Thus, this thesis became, to the best of my knowledge, the first book-length survey of the science-fiction film in the English language.[1]

With the 1960's a few films of much higher quality began to appear (of which, more later), along with a great increase in popular and academic interest in motion pictures in general. As a result, film books of all sorts, so scarce during the 50's, now began to proliferate. But still there was only an occasional brief mention here and there of the history and/or significance of the science-fiction film. The chief references to such films continued to be found only in magazines and newspapers. *Famous Monsters of Filmland*, a periodical

---

[1] I make this qualification because, years later, I discovered the existence of an obscure French paperback history: Jacques Siclier and André S. Labarthe, *Images de la Science-Fiction* (Paris: Les Éditions du Cerf, 1958), 137 pp. To my knowledge, an English-language edition has not yet been published.

devoted to monster movies of all kinds, was started in 1958 by editor Forrest J Ackerman and is still going strong today. It spawned a host of imitations, most of which died out within a few years, but even FM's coverage of science-fiction films has always been on a rather juvenile level, like that of the horror and monster movies.[2]

But even with the increased interest in horror films, it was not until 1967 that the first good book on the subject was published in this country. Carlos Clarens's An Illustrated History of the Horror Film (New York: Putnam, 1967, 256 pp.) was well received critically and remains the finest single reference to date on the horror film in general. An entire chapter is devoted to the science-fiction film, but while well written, it is necessarily brief.

So, it was not until 1970--over a decade after this thesis was written--that the first book devoted entirely to the science-fiction film finally appeared. Science Fiction in the Cinema was published simultaneously in paperback in both Britain and the United States (New York: A. S. Barnes/London: A. Zwemmer, 240 pp.) and was the work of John Baxter, an Australian science-fiction writer. It is a handsome little book, well written and researched, and copiously illustrated with stills, many quite rare. It provides interesting information on hundreds of s-f films, tracing their themes and trends from Georges Méliès' A Trip to the Moon (1902) to Stanley Kubrick's 2001: A Space Odyssey (1968). It includes a brief bibliography and select filmography, giving casts and credits for more than 150 important films. It is highly recommended.

In 1971 another book appeared, also published simultaneously in Britain and the U.S., written by Denis Gifford, an Englishman who has authored several books on the horror film. Science Fiction Film (London: Studio Vista/New York: Dutton, 160 pp.) was published in both hardcover and paperback editions, and is also an excellent reference. More a survey than an analytical or critical examination, this book provides brief comments on over 500 films, grouped into categories such as "The Machine," "The Aeroplane," "The Robot," "The Ray," and the like. An index of film titles is included, and there are many excellent stills, with very little duplication of those in the Baxter book.

Although these two volumes are the only ones beside the

---

[2] Interestingly enough, in 1961 Ackerman attempted to launch a companion magazine devoted entirely to a more serious approach to the s-f film. It was called Spacemen and folded from lack of reader support after only nine issues, thereby demonstrating vividly the enormously greater popularity of horror and monster films. Today there is only one good professional magazine in this country devoted to serious study of fantasy and s-f films, Cinefantastique, a handsome, slick-paper periodical, published quarterly.

present work to cover s-f film history, mention should be ma
of a third book, published in 1972, which is also an intere
ing reference. Focus on the Science Fiction Film (Englewoo
Cliffs, New Jersey: Prentice-Hall, New Jersey, 182 pp.) is a
anthology of commentaries, essays, interviews and other pie
dealing with the science-fiction film, past and present, edi
ed by William Johnson. Of particular interest is a section
of interviews with a number of established science-fiction
writers and filmmakers, who give their views on s-f films.
Included are: Brian Aldiss, Isaac Asimov, Anthony Burgess,
John W. Campbell, Jr., Arthur C. Clarke, Robert A. Heinlein
and Fritz Lang. A small section of stills is included in
this volume, along with a filmography, bibliography and ind

Finally, there are now available two extremely importa
checklists, invaluable to anyone interested in the s-f film
for any reason. The first is Horror and Science Fiction Fil
A Checklist (Metuchen, New Jersey: Scarecrow Press, 1972, 61
pp.) by Donald C. Willis. This one-volume hardcover work l
over 4,000 horror and s-f films, giving synopses of most of
them, along with casts, credits, dates, etc. It is an excel
lent reference, but unfortunately, is completely overshadow
by the second, and by far the most valuable, work, Walter L
monumental three-volume Reference Guide to Fantastic Films
(Los Angeles: Chelsea-Lee Books, 1972/1973/1974, 691 pp.).
Published in a sturdy, 8½" x 11" paperbound format, this lo
awaited work is a staggeringly impressive mass of informati
on some 20,000 science-fiction, fantasy and horror films fr
all over the world, illustrated with many rare stills. It
the result of many years of painstaking research, an almost
unbelievable labor of love, and I cannot recommend or prais
it too highly. It is easily the greatest single contributi
to research on the science-fiction film (and the horror and
fantasy film also) ever published.

With the publication of such new and important referen
on the science-fiction film comes the recognition of a rath
painful responsibility which I, as author of this thesis,
feel I should meet in order to make the work of optimum val
within its limitations, to the researcher. To explain:

During the decade since this thesis was written, I hav
in the course of continued research come across a large bod
of information which was not available to me in the 50's.
This information has made me sadly aware of a number of omi
sions and errors in the text, which I can only ascribe to
youth, inexperience and lack of time (the entire project wa
completed between January and May of 1959), but which nevertheless impair the usefulness of this work as a research to
I had hoped to be able to completely revise and correct the
book and perhaps bring it up to date in detail before publication, but this has proved to be impossible.

When the decision was made to reprint this thesis as
part of the Arno Press Science-Fiction Series, it was under-

stood that the book, like the others in the series, would be reprinted as is, without additions or corrections. Therefore, the original text of this work has not been altered.

However, since this is not just a new edition of a work published previously (theses and dissertations are considered "unpublished works"), but actually constitutes first publication, the publishers have generously allowed me to add this introduction and a much-needed index of film titles, for which I am grateful.

In the introduction, therefore, I have tried to accomplish three main objectives: first, to bring to the readers' attention the most important reference works in the field of the s-f film published since 1959, in lieu of updating the bibliography and the review of literature in Chapter II; second, to correct some of the more glaring errors in the text (omissions will have to wait for a second and hopefully completely revised edition); and third, to briefly recap what has happened to the science-fiction film in the decade since 1959 and bring the reader up to date with the 70's.

The following, then, are the most important errata that I have had time to catch and correct prior to publication:

1) The correct title of the serial mentioned on page 26 as _Diamond in the Sky_ is _The Diamond from the Sky_.

2) The film I have listed as _Air Hawks_ (1925) on page 32 was really called _The Air Hawk_ and is not s-f, although the 1935 _Air Hawks_ is (p. 49).

3) _The Thirteenth Moon of Jupiter_ (p. 115) is the original (British) title of the film released in this country as _Fire Maidens of Outer Space_ (p. 119), and not a separate film.

4) The correct title of the Three Stooges short mentioned on page 141 as _Outer Space Daze_ is _Outer Space Jitters_.

5) The Czech film, _War with the Newts_ (p. 142), was apparently not made in 1958. It was announced in production again in 1966, but to date has not been released.

6) The Italian production of another Karel Čapek work, _R. U. R._ (pp. 142 and 154), was never made; however, there was an earlier film produced in Russia called _Gibel Sensatsy_ (_Loss of Sensation_)(1935), which seems to be based to some extent on the Čapek play, in that a scientist invents a robot that turns on him and kills him.

7) The following films have been determined not science fiction, despite misleading titles: _Avant le Deluge_ (_Before the Deluge_), _The Forty-Ninth Man_, _Operation X_, _Project X_,[3] _Run for the Hills_, _Sword of Venus_ and _World for Ransom_.

8) The female robot in _Metropolis_ was not really "the

---

[3]This is the 1949 _Project X_ (p. 72); another _Project X_, which definitely _is_ science-fiction, was released by Paramount in 1967.

screen's first robot," as I stated on page 34, although she was the first famous one, and probably the first one to properly bear the new name "robot," given to us by Karel Čapek in his 1922 play, _R. U. R._ Denis Gifford lists at least 15 films featuring various types of robots prior to 1926,[4] although they were then called "mechanical men," "clockwork men," or "automata." Gifford states that the first screen "mechanical man" appeared in an 1897 film by Georges Méliès, _Gugusse et l'Automate_ (_The Clown and the Automaton_). Which brings up an interesting point, and my final erratum.

Speaking of Méliès, most film historians seem to agree on his _A Trip to the Moon_ (1902) as the first real science-fiction film. I had listed another Méliès film, _Hydrothérapie fantastique ou le Secret du Docteur_ (_Fantastic Hydrotherapy or The Doctor's Secret_) (p. 20) as having been made earlier, in 1900, but subsequent research has proven my original source for this date to be incorrect. Méliès did not produce this film until 1909.[5]

However, to complicate matters, he did produce several other films prior to 1902 that contain elements, at least, of what can be called science fiction: _Gugusse et l'Automate_ (1897), featuring the automaton mentioned above; _Les rayons Roentgen_ (_The X-Rays_; _A Novice at X-Rays_)(1898), which deals with the newly-discovered (1895) marvel in a comic fantasy manner; and _Coppélia ou La poupée animée_ (_Coppélia or The Animated Doll_) (1900), based on the Delibes ballet from the E. T. A. Hoffmann story, "The Sand-Man," and featuring a dancing female automaton.

To further confuse the issue, during this same period other filmmakers were busy producing films like these: _The X-Ray Fiend_ or _X-Rays_ (George Smith, 1897), a British variation on the Roentgen theme which has a professor's machine reveal the embracing skeletons of two lovers; _The Sausage Machine_ (Biograph, 1897), in which dogs are made into sausages; _Making Sausages_ (George Smith, 1898), a British "improvement" on the Biograph recipe with cats, ducks and old boots; _La Poupée_ (_The Doll_), another French version of the Hoffmann story, "The Sand-Man," this time as interpreted in an opera by Edmond Audran; and _La machine volante_ (_The Flying Machine_), also known as _À la Conquête_

---

[4]Denis Gifford, _Science Fiction Film_ (London: Studio Vista; New York: Dutton, 1971), pp. 51-53.

[5]Georges Sadoul, _Georges Méliès_ (Paris: Éditions Seghers, 1961), p. 220.

de l'Air (The Conquest of the Air), (Pathé, 1901) in which French director Ferdinand Zecca has a man riding a kind of bicycle-airship through the sky.

So the question remains: What is the first true science-fiction film and who made it when? Those content to grant the honor to Méliès may be on shaky ground, for even his Trip to the Moon may have been preceded by an earlier lunar voyage: On a playbill for the Court Theatre, New Road, Brighton, England, said to have been distributed about 1900, is the notice: "From Earth to Moon: The Latest Fantastic Picture."[6] I can find no other reference anywhere to this one.

Researching films in this early period is extremely difficult, as little remains of many of them except a title and a line or two of description; but perhaps some day some intrepid historian will be able to definitely establish the identity of the world's first science-fiction film. Until then, I think we can in all fairness allow Méliès to keep his well-earned title of "Father of the Science-Fiction Film."

So much for the errata; there may be more I haven't caught, so I hereby invite communication from readers with information of any kind about s-f films, in care of the publishers, Arno Press.

Now, to bring us up to date:

Since 1959, science-fiction films have come a long way toward maturity, both in execution and in content. The hope that I optimistically expressed in the last chapter of this work (p. 157) has been largely fulfilled, although it has taken filmmakers nearly a decade to do it.

As we struggled through the turbulent 60's, gradually a few good films began to emerge from the continuing welter of low-budget "creature" films that had saturated the last half of the 50's: On the Beach (1959), an intelligent adaptation of the Nevil Shute novel, directed by Stanley Kramer; George Pal's The Time Machine (1960), solidly based on H. G. Wells's 1895 classic; Village of the Damned (1960), top screenwriter Stirling Silliphant's adaptation of John Wyndham's novel, The Midwich Cuckoos; Joseph Losey's shocking The Damned (1961), produced by Hammer Films and released in the U.S. as These Are the Damned; the brilliant animated short, Icarus Montgolfier Wright (1962), based on a short story by Ray Bradbury and nominated for an Academy Award; La Jetée (The Jetty; The Pier)(1962) an intriguing French experiment in time travel utilizing still photographs; Ikaria XB-1 (1963), the much-acclaimed Czech film released in the U.S. as Voyage to the End of the Universe; the superb and chilling Lord of the

---

[6] Rachel Low and Roger Manvell, The History of the British Film: 1896-1906 (Vol. I) (London: George Allen and Unwin, 1948), plate 12.

Flies (1963), written and directed by Peter Brook from the novel by William Golding; Dr. Strangelove or: How I Learned to Stop Worrying and Love the Bomb (1963), Stanley Kubrick's memorable black comedy and his first venture into science fiction and a number of others, happily too numerous to mention here.

Even the s-f films made solely to entertain showed imagination and style: Journey to the Center of the Earth (1959) was a dazzling CinemaScope romp through Jules Verne's subterranean wonders; Master of the World (1961), another amalgam of Verne from scriptwriter Richard Matheson, featured Vincent Price as an airborne Captain Nemo named Robur; and a new version of H. G. Wells's First Men in the Moon (1964) displayed some of Ray Harryhausen's finest special effects.

Besides the films mentioned above, the year 1963 brought an event of great importance to the science-fiction film: the first annual International Science-Fiction Film Festival was held at Trieste, thereby demonstrating the increasing interest in s-f films all over the world. Sadly, the best the U.S. could think to offer was Bert I. Gordon's unoriginal Attack of the Puppet People (1958) and Roger Corman's pretentious X--The Man with X-Ray Eyes (1963).

During the latter half of the 60's, things got even better. Now, for the first time since the early 50's, important producers, directors and actors were being attracted to and intrigued by the possibilities of the science-fiction film; color and wide screen were adding important dimensions of visual excitement, and intelligent scripts were presenting interesting and challenging concepts to a more mature audience. Jean-Luc Godard's Alphaville (1965) was an original if not altogether successful satire of science fiction and detective films; Ray Bradbury's long-awaited Fahrenheit 451 (1966) was brought to the screen by another Frenchman, François Truffaut, starring Julie Christie and Oskar Werner; the Russians contributed Tumannost' Andromedy (The Andromeda Nebula)(1967), from the novel by Soviet s-f writer Ivan Efremov; Fantastic Voyage (1966) was a stunning tour-de-force of special effects for a journey through a human bloodstream; Jane Fonda appeared as Barbarella (1967), the space-traveling heroine of Jean-Claude Forest's adult French comic strip; the last (and best) of the Quatermass trilogy[7] finally reached us as Five Million Years to Earth (Quatermass and the Pit in England) (1967); and George Lucas, a student at USC, made an outstanding short film, THX-1138-4EB (1967), which was to become the nucleus of a feature film a few years later and start him on the road to an important directorial career.

---

[7]For the first two films in this series, see The Creeping Unknown (1956) (pp. 125-126, 135) and Enemy from Space (1956) (pp. 126-127).

And then came 1968--perhaps the most significant year in the history of the science-fiction film since 1902--the year in which s-f films finally proved that they could hold their own with any other type of film in terms of maturity, excellence of production--and even box office success. This was the year that saw the first Academy Award ever won by an actor in a science-fiction film go to Cliff Robertson for his sensitive performance in Charly, based on Flowers for Algernon by Daniel Keyes. This was the year that gave us the first of the enormously popular "Apes" films, Planet of the Apes, adapted by Rod Serling from the novel by Pierre Boulle. This film has spawned four sequels, paperback novelizations, comic books, model kits, and now a TV series! But most important, 1968 was the year that brought us what many have called the best science-fiction film ever made--Stanley Kubrick's and Arthur C. Clarke's monumental 2001: A Space Odyssey.

Much has been written about this film in books, magazines and newspapers--perhaps more than has ever been written about any single s-f film before. In fact, several books devoted entirely to 2001 have been published, including the novelization by Arthur C. Clarke himself. Boasting a budget of millions and filmed in utmost secrecy in Cinerama, this amazing spectacle has proved enormously successful at the box office despite a tremendous polarization of critical opinion, and thus has done a great deal toward hastening the maturity of the s-f film. Producers began to realize that s-f films could make money if done with generous budgets and intelligent, literate scripts; for whatever the faults of 2001 may be, it is a film to make you think. It offers no easy answers, and people find themselves returning to experience it again and again. It is not easily forgotten.

And so, 1969 saw the expansion of a new renaissance in intelligent, big-budget s-f films: Journey to the Far Side of the Sun, the first feature of Sylvia and Gerry Anderson, producers of such popular British TV series as Thunderbirds and Stingray, combined superb models, miniatures, puppets and live actors in an intriguing story; Marooned, a taut, suspenseful drama of astronauts in trouble, starred Gregory Peck and Gene Hackman; Colossus: The Forbin Project was made from D. F. Jones's novel about a gigantic computer that takes over the world; The Bed Sitting Room was an hilariously surreal British comedy by Spike Milligan and Richard Lester about the incredible goings-on after World War III; and THX 1138, George Lucas's expansion of his 1967 short film, was an uneven but still effective look at an underground dystopia of the future.

Nineteen sixty-nine also brought us another kind of big-budget production, as the cinematic fantasies of Georges Méliès, Fritz Lang and George Pal became fact: man walked on the moon for the first time! This long-dreamed-of feat also helped to bring the worlds of science fiction closer to public awareness, so that the opening years of the 70's have seen science fict and the s-f film reach a peak of great popularity.

Since 1970, we have seen an encouraging number of outst ing s-f films, and the end is not in sight. No Blade of Gra (1970) was produced and directed by Cornel Wilde from the ec logical nightmare novel of John Christopher; Omega (1970) wa a short experimental UCLA film by Donald Fox, loosely based part of Arthur C. Clarke's Childhood's End, and an impressiv display of homemade special effects; Beneath the Planet of t Apes (1971) was the first of five sequels to the 1968 film; The Andromeda Strain (1971) was produced and directed by Rob Wise from the best-seller by Michael Crichton; Kurt Vonnegut sardonic trip in time and space, Slaughterhouse-Five (1971), directed by George Roy Hill; Escape from the Planet of the A (1971)ingeniously continued the series after the complete de tion of the earth in the second film (!); Stanley Kubrick's venture into science fiction was Anthony Burgess's A Clockwo Orange (1971), a brilliant and brutal study in "ultraviolenc and "rehabilitation" in the not-too-distant future; Silent Running (1971) was a disappointing but visually fascinating film by Douglas Trumbull, who engineered many of the special effects of 2001 and The Andromeda Strain; Between Time and Timbuktu or Prometheus-5 (1972) was a superb black comedy ba on the works of Kurt Vonnegut, Jr., filmed for National Educ tional Television; Russia produced Stanislas Lem's internati ally-acclaimed novel, Solaris (1972); Michael Crichton direc his Westworld (1973), a chilling look at modern technology g mad; Edward G. Robinson played his last role in Soylent Gree (1973), another future nightmare, based on Harry Harrison's novel Make Room! Make Room!; John Boorman's controversial an enigmatic Zardoz (1973) starred ex-007 Sean Connery; Battle the Planet of the Apes (1973) was the fifth and final (?) "A film; Mike Nichols's bleak look at man's inhumanity to other species--and his own, The Day of the Dolphin (1973), starred George C. Scott and some beautiful dolphins; The Spook Who S by the Door (1973)portrayed a terrifying black revolution against the U.S.; La Planète Sauvage (The Savage Planet)(197 was a French-Czech co-production, the first full-length anim s-f film, and won the Grand Prix at the 1973 Cannes Film Fes tival. It was released in this country as Fantastic Planet. Nineteen seventy-three ended with Sleeper, Woody Allen's hil ous romp through the world of tomorrow, and Chariots of the Gods? a feature-length documentary based on the controversia books by Erich von Däniken, produced in West Germany in 1969 as Erinnerungen an die Zukunft (Memories of the Future).

When we compare these films of the past decade with tho being produced in 1959 we can see the tremendous strides tha have been made. Quality has replaced quantity; the works of established science fiction authors are being filmed; import filmmakers are working with science fiction, and relevant, thought-provoking concepts dealing with man's relationship t himself and his environment, today and tomorrow, are being handled in an adult and visually exciting manner. We can only hope that this encouraging and gratifying trend will continue into the second half of the 70's. I believe it will.

Douglas Menville

Los Angeles
September, 1974

CHAPTER I

THE PROBLEM AND DEFINITIONS OF TERMS USED

With the recent and alarming launching of the Soviet and American space satellites, it has been brought home with sudden and convincing reality that we stand on the threshold of the Space Age. In the past, the exploration and conquest of outer space has merely provided material for speculative fiction-writers and science articles. Today fact is treading hard upon the heels of fancy; everywhere is an increasing awareness of the ever-mushrooming role that science is playing in shaping our thinking, our behavior, and our very survival.

This growing awareness of, and interest in, science has been reflected by all of the media of mass communication, particularly in the realm of entertainment. The use of science combined with fiction is generally called "science-fiction," a term which is not new to story-telling. It provides the writer and the reader with the one form of literature in which there are no apparent limits to the imagination, except those imposed by physical laws of which we are presently cognizant. If a writer ventures beyond these boundaries and writes of something which we generally agree could not occur, such as the manifestation of supernatural or metaphysical beings, he is no longer in the realm of science-fiction, but has invaded that of "fantasy." But so long as the writer confines his imagination to that which is at least possible, based on physical laws as we know them, he is writing "science-fiction," no matter how improbable it may seem. This gives his writing a validity that fantasy cannot achieve, and is one reason why science-fiction can be a powerful means of education and social criticism. Here, the fantastic is based on science, not sorcery.

Film is peculiarly well adapted to the portrayal of science-fiction in a stimulating, informative and educational manner through imaginative and ingenious uses of technical devices and artistic techniques. Unfortunately, however, the science-fiction film often neglects, to an alarming degree, the elements of story and acting. In the opinions of many moviegoers and almost all critics, it has tended—especially in recent years—to concentrate on the sensational, horrifying and shocking aspects of science. The increased scientific awareness has provided a ready market for such low-budget thrillers, which have reduced the science-fiction film to the level of slavish duplication and an almost complete lack of originality—and originality is one of the chief virtues of this field. During the last few years the science-fiction film, with its emphasis on violence and scientific absurdities, has become something which critics deplore, adult cinemagoers accept with little or no enthusiasm and teen-agers flock to *en masse*. As can be seen from any recent survey, the largest portion of today's film audience consists of teen-agers.

While critical, the plight of the science-fiction film is not hopeless. Its past suggests its potential for imaginative and adult ideas, entertainingly and tastefully presented. The answers to what can be done to restore it to a respectable cinematic position are not readily evident. Some of them lie buried in the history of the science-fiction film, which can be traced back to the turn of the century.

I. THE PROBLEM

Statement of the problem. It was the purpose of this study (1) to provide an organized body of historical and critical information on the science-fiction film, chronologically arranged; (2) to utilize this material in setting up certain criteria for judging the artistic and technical standards of films of this type; and (3) to apply these criteria in an evaluation of current science-fiction film production.

Importance of the problem. The almost total absence of literature on the science-fiction film suggests that extensive investigation is long overdue. It was also felt that a better appreciation of the science-fiction film can only be obtained by a survey of the assets and liabilities of past films as compared with those of today. This thesis has attempted to include every film on which the writer could find information, and aims to create a sharper awareness of the role of the science-fiction film in the history of cinema.

II. DEFINITIONS OF TERMS USED

The term "science-fiction" has been much abused in its application to both literature and film because it is by its very nature difficult to define accurately. Particularly in regard to film, this term has been used by critics and the public as an all-inclusive one to cover a number of films more accurately placed in the categories of "horror" or "fantasy." Admittedly, any classification of films into specific groups must, in the last analysis, be largely a matter of personal opinion. Nevertheless, the term "science-fiction" as used in this thesis was applied to any film with an extrapolative scientific basis upon which a story was constructed, as opposed to films with a predominately supernatural or mysterious basis or mood. The science-fiction film is based on speculation as to what could or will possibly occur, given a valid scientific premise. To extrapolate on this premise, the film-maker enlarges upon it, speculates upon what could conceivably occur, no matter how improbable it may seem. Science-fiction is still fiction, not fact, so the licenses of fiction are applicable, but it is based on facts as we know them. Therefore, if in a film some sort of scientific reasoning or explanation was given for a set of extraordinary phenomena, as opposed to an explanation based on legend or supernaturalism, the film was considered to be "science-fiction."

As opposed to this, the "fantasy" film would include all other types of film in which the bizarre, the unearthly, the supernatural occurs, and is either not explained or explained in supernatural, legendary or occult terms. The Wizard of Oz is a fantasy film under this definition, as is Dracula.

The "horror" film is actually a sub-category under "fantasy," but should be considered separately in view of its wide usage and the tendency of many horror films to be confused with science-fiction films, because of the employment by the latter of many of the elements of the former. These elements, in addition to conforming to those of any fantasy film, cause the horror film to stand out as a separate type of film. Emphasis in the horror film is upon those elements of story, acting, direction, photography, sound and editing which horrify, frighten and shock. The entire approach of a horror film is one of stimulating terror, a desire to appeal to that part of us which thrills to the unknown, the supernatural and the grotesque. One could not call The Wizard of Oz a horror film, but Dracula would certainly fall under this classification, since it contains the elements peculiar to the horror film, as well as those of the fantasy film.

Another important consideration in the classification of films included in this thesis was the question of general approach, atmosphere, and mood of a film. Aside from subject matter, if the approach to a given film was that of the horror film, the film was considered as such, even though it may have contained some scientific elements. For example, a film like Frankenstein, although based upon "scientific" experimentation with lightning, was considered a horror film because of its general approach and techniques of production, while a film like The Thing was classified as science-fiction because it dealt with an extra-terrestial being, although it contained strong "horror" elements. Based as much as possible on the above definitions, these classifications still remain somewhat arbitrary.

The final consideration in classifying films for this study was that of degree. Many films, such as I'll Never Forget You, Dick Tracy Meets Gruesome, and King Kong, contain only small amounts of scientific speculation or include merely a science-fiction "gimmick" or two in their plots, without which they would fall into some other category, such as gangster, musical or comedy. Examples of such gimmicks would be the atomic explosion which irradiates Mickey Rooney in The Atomic Kid, or the "cyclotrode" in The Crimson Ghost. Whenever the science-fiction element was deemed essential to the plot of the film, the film was included as science-fiction.

In general it was evident that most of the films considered fell readily into either science-fiction or horror categories, with difficulties in classification arising only with such borderline cases as King Kong, Breaking the Sound Barrier and a few others. Whenever one of these borderline films was included, the writer has attempted to add comments justifying its inclusion.

Limitations of the study. Until the last two or three years, the number of films that fell into the purely "science-fiction" category were relatively few, compared to the number of those in the "horror" and "fantasy" categories. For that reason it was not thought necessary to limit the study to an arbitrary starting date. However, due to three factors, it was thought prudent to conclude the study with the year 1957. These factors were: (1) 1957 marked the year in which the current increase in science-fiction films had about reached its peak; (2) the pictures, with a few exceptions, seemed to level off in uniformity of production and subject matter, with no significant changes in films produced in 1958 or the first part of 1959; and (3) this marked the year in which a trend toward strictly "horror" films began to manifest itself, causing them to outnumber the "science-fiction" films. Further, it was not thought necessary to limit the films considered to those made in the United States, since some of the best-known films in the genre were of foreign origin. However, the majority of films considered will necessarily be American, especially the more recent ones, since the United States has always maintained the lead in producing science-fiction pictures. Finally, it was thought to limit the study to include only films classified by this writer into the science-fiction category, excluding any discussion of horror or fantasy films. The horror and fantasy film in America has been covered thoroughly in a thesis written in 1953,[1] although there is still room for research on the foreign horror film.

[1]Jack Nealon, "An Historical and Critical Survey of the American Horror Film Since 1930" (unpublished Master's thesis, The University of Southern California, Los Angeles, 1953).

CHAPTER II

REVIEW OF THE LITERATURE

AND METHODS OF PROCEDURE

I. REVIEW OF THE LITERATURE

As has been stated previously, the writer has been unable to uncover any satisfactory book-length treatment of science-fiction in film. There are passages in several books, however, which deal with the science-fiction film, and occasionally whole chapters. There is a book-length treatment in preparation at the present time, but this study will in all probability not be finished before the completion of this thesis.[1] Most of the available material on the science-fiction film is to be found in magazines and newspapers, in the form of articles and reviews. Especially helpful in obtaining lists and dates of films were two reference books, The Film Daily Year Book and the International Motion Picture Almanac. The only published work of recent interest is

---

[1] Mr. Walter W. Lee, Jr., is currently compiling data for his forthcoming book, tentatively entitled Science Fiction and Fantasy Films: A History, according to a report prepared for a cinema class at the University of Southern California by Mr. Richard Tuber. This report, "A Quantitative Analysis of Science Fiction Films, 1945-1957," contains a great deal of information from Mr. Lee's files, and this writer is indebted to this report. Acknowledgment is also made to a tentative bibliography and an extensive checklist of science-fiction

a new volume from France, Le Fantastique au Cinéma, by Michel Laclos,[2] which contains some interesting information on the science-fiction film, despite the fact that it is largely a picture-book and concerns itself primarily with the fantasy film. In a review of this book in the British film periodical Sight and Sound, the reviewer supports the findings of this writer regarding material on the science-fiction film:

> Always excepting occasional observations in such publications as Anthony Boucher's Magazine of Fantasy and Science Fiction, and isolated reviews and articles in film magazines, not many fantastic movies receive anything but condescension and sociological sniping until they are twenty years old. As many of them are also extremely fugitive items in the first place, there is a lack both of documentation concerning them and of a context in which to place them critically: therefore Laclos' book . . . surveys science fiction movies and their links with earlier horror films, and ends with an appeal for closer and more sympathetic study of the directors, writers, and stars of fantasy films.[3]

II. METHODS OF PROCEDURE

Sources of data. For the purposes of this study, the writer was fortunate in having seen over the years a large percentage of the films with which the study is concerned. Therefore this investigation was

---

and fantasy films which Mr. Lee compiled for his book.

[2]Michel Laclos, Le Fantastique au Cinéma (Paris: Jean-Jacques Pauvert, 1958), 197 pp. Illustrated.

[3]Roy Edwards, "Book Reviews," Sight and Sound, Autumn, 1958, p. 326.

not handicapped by the risk of writing about unseen films, which is often the case in appraisals of early motion pictures. In addition, the writer had access to an extensive personal file of clippings, articles, stills and reviews on the science-fiction film, collected over a period of about fifteen years. Other criticisms and synopses of the films were taken from articles and reviews in film histories, magazines, and newspapers. These materials have been secured from the University of Southern California Library, the Los Angeles Public Library, the library of the Academy of Motion Picture Arts and Sciences, and from the writer's own collections. Information was also obtained through a personal interview with the late Henry Kuttner, science-fiction novelist, short-story writer and screenwriter.

Organization of the remainder of the thesis. Utilizing these materials, the writer has attempted to present an overall history of the science-fiction film in the subsequent chapters. Chapter Four will be an examination of the science-fiction film in general, weighing its collective vices and virtues, and comparing current standards of production with those of past years. Chapter Five will be a summary and set of conclusions based upon the content of the preceding chapters.

CHAPTER III

THE HISTORY OF SCIENCE-FICTION IN FILM

Science-fiction itself, as a form of literature, can be traced back in history as far as approximately 150 A. D. Most authorities agree that the Greek satirist Lucian of Samosata was the first man to pen a story of scientific speculation. His True History recounts a trip to the moon and provides an elaborate discussion of its inhabitants and their mores. They were

> . . . bald, bearded moon people with stomach pouches and removable eyes. Their airborne cavalry flew into battle wearing giant pea pods for helmets.[1]

Similar accounts of lunar travel were written by the great astronomer Johann Kepler, whose story Somnium appeared first in 1638, and by Ariosto, whose Orlando Furioso in 1532 told of beings who disappeared from earth and showed up on the moon. Tommaso Campanella wrote a classic utopian work, The City of the Sun (1623) and appears as a character in a later work by Cyrano de Bergerac. In 1638, a volume entitled The Man in the Moone: or a Discourse of a Voyage Thither was published by British Bishop Francis Godwin.

---

[1]"The Moon: Myths, Marvels and Man's Reach for It," Life, December 15, 1958, p. 92.

> . . . as part of the story, his hero, Domingo Gonsales, travels to the moon with birds serving as the motive power for a contraption he has built.[2]

On the moon, Gonsales encountered moon folk who got around by leaping up in the air and fanning themselves along. All of these previous works had been studied intently by the great poet, swordsman, philosopher, playwright and acolyte of science, Cyrano de Bergerac. Cyrano's brilliant speculation and imagination gained him the position of the 17th century's greatest science-fiction writer, and his Voyage to the Moon, written in 1648, was the most soundly scientific science-fiction story of the period. This work, his most famous,

> . . . went into nine editions in France and two translations into English between the years 1650 and 1687. Previous to its publication it was extensively circulated in manuscript form, and read by many of his more distinguished contemporaries.
>
> Unlike other romancers, utopians and satirists of the period, who wrote occasional works of primitive science fiction as a convenient means of forwarding a particular political or social concept, de Bergerac persisted in his literary endeavors and wrote a sequel to A Voyage to the Moon entitled A Voyage to the Sun. The story, although apparently incomplete, was no mere fragment, for it exceeded in length A Voyage to the Moon. A third science fiction novel, the Story of the Spark, is referred to in contemporary writings, but the actual manuscript was stolen and has never been found.
>
> . . . .
>
> In A Voyage to the Moon, de Bergerac's hero spends weeks experimenting on a space ship, several models failing to get off the ground. Success crowns his efforts when some Canadians tie

---

[2] Sam Moskowitz, "Cyrano de Bergerac: Swordsman of Space," Satellite Science Fiction, March, 1959, p. 34.

rockets to his space shell and he is fired aloft.[3]

High in the atmosphere, the rockets give out, but fortunately Cyrano had rubbed himself with bone marrow, to ease the bruises of a previously unsuccessful flight. Since it was popularly believed in Cyrano's time that the sun sucked up bone marrow, our hero was carried by this method through space, ultimately to land on the moon.

The moon turns out to be inhabited by humanoid creatures that go about on all fours. However, it is interesting to note that Cyrano makes a point of stressing the light gravitational pull of the moon, by relating how the inhabitants are able to 'fan' themselves through the air.

In his two novels, Cyrano makes seven different suggestions for defying gravity to reach the moon . . . ![4]

Cyrano, although wildly inaccurate at times, showed an amazing gift of prophecy, for he foretold such inventions as the radiant light bulb, the phonograph, the ram-jet, and came close to the internal combustion engine; he observed that the earth and the other planets revolve around the sun and that the sun is the center of the solar system,[5] and speculated on the existence of atoms and psychosomatic illnesses.

After Cyrano came many imitators, such as Tom d'Urfy's work,

---

[3]Thus Cyrano invented the first "rocket ship"—he was the first man to think of rockets as a propellant medium for a space craft.

[4]Moskowitz, op. cit., pp. 32, 33-34.

[5]Lest this be regarded as an elementary observation, it should be remembered that only sixteen years before the publication of Cyrano's statement, Galileo was forced by the Inquisition to recant this same observation, which his telescopes had confirmed, as a

Wonders in the Sun or The Kingdom of the Birds, published in London in 1706. Used as the basis of an opera, it was a direct steal from Cyrano, even to the use of his characters. Moon serpents who spoke English were created in 1793 by an unknown writer with the pen name Aratus. His hero reached the moon in a balloon "in exactly 17 days, six hours, two minutes, three seconds."[6] Bernardin de St. Pierre wrote in the 17th century of Martian warriors, and the great satirist Jonathan Swift was influenced a great deal by Cyrano's writings. In Gulliver's Travels, Book III (1726), he predicts the two moons of Mars, encounters a group of immortals, and visits a strange floating island, which is supported and propelled by a giant lodestone:

> By means of this loadstone, the island is made to rise and fall, and move from one place to another. For with respect to that part of the earth over which the monarch presides, the stone is endued at one of its sides with an attractive power, and at the other with a repulsive. Upon placing the magnet erect with its attracting end towards the earth, the island descends; but when the repelling extremity points downwards, the island mounts directly upwards. When the position of the stone is oblique, the motion of the island is too. For in this magnet the forces always act in lines parallel to its direction.[7]

Great writers of all ages have turned toward science-fiction as a means of expressing their feelings on philosophy, religion, customs

---

"heresy."

[6] "The Moon: Myths, Marvels and Man's Reach for It," op. cit., p. 93.

[7] Jonathan Swift, Gulliver's Travels (New York: Random House, 1950), pp. 190-191.

and mores, finding it a fertile field in which to plant the seeds of satire and social reform. The French satirist Voltaire wrote, like Swift, of the twin moons of Mars, and one of his works, Micromegas, concerned a visitor from another star. An angel provided the transportation for the hero of George Fowler's A Flight to the Moon in 1813. Writers such as Samuel Butler, Sir Thomas More, Edward Bellamy, Edgar Allan Poe and C. S. Lewis paved the way for the adventurous tales of Jules Verne and the more serious sociological fantasies of H. G. Wells.

Verne's powers of prediction were extraordinary. In his many novels, he predicted the submarine, the airplane, the television-phone, the talking picture, the helicopter, supersonic speed, solar energy, television, and countless other developments which we have seen come true in our own lifetimes. Many of his stories have been filmed, some several times. Twenty Thousand Leagues Under the Sea has been made three times; The Mysterious Island twice, with another version in production now; Around the World in 80 Days has been lavishly treated on both stage and screen; and A Journey to the Center of the Earth is also in production.

H. G. Wells has been treated well by the movies also. The Invisible Man, The Island of Dr. Moreau, The Shape of Things to Come, "The Man Who Could Work Miracles" (a short story), and The War of the Worlds have all been transferred to the screen. George Pal is currently in production on The Time Machine. Wells' prophetic accuracy was remarkable also, but not to the degree of Verne's. He wrote of his work:

> These tales have been compared with the work of Jules Verne and there was a disposition on the part of literary journalists at one time to call me the English Jules Verne. As a matter of fact there is no literary resemblance whatever between the anticipatory inventions of the great Frenchman and these fantasies. His work dealt almost always with actual possibilities of invention and discovery, and he made some remarkable forecasts. The interest he invoked was a practical one; he wrote and believed and told that this or that thing could be done, which was not at that time done. He helped his reader to imagine it done and to realise what fun, excitement, or mischief would ensue. Many of his inventions have "come true." But these stories of mine collected here do not pretend to deal with possible things; they are exercises of the imagination in a quite different field. They belong to a class of writing which includes the Golden Ass of Apuleius, the True Histories of Lucian, Peter Schlemil and the story of Frankenstein. . . . They are all fantasies; they do not aim to project a serious possibility; they aim indeed only at the same amount of conviction as one gets in a good gripping dream. . . .
>
> In all this type of story the living interest lies in their non-fantastic elements and not in the invention itself. They are appeals for human sympathy quite as much as any "sympathetic" novel, and the fantastic element, the strange property or the strange world, is used only to throw up and intensify our natural reactions of wonder, fear or perplexity.[8]

In 1926, the first magazine devoted entirely to scientific fiction, or "scientifiction," as it was then called, was put on the newsstands. It was called Amazing Stories, and is still being published today. An immediate success, its early issues featured stories by H. G. Wells, Jules Verne, Edgar Allan Poe, Olaf Stapledon, Edgar Rice Burroughs,

---

[8] H. G. Wells, "Preface," Seven Famous Novels (Garden City, New York: Garden City, 1934), p. vii.

and many others. After this, the deluge—the science-fiction field mushroomed enormously until today it has invaded all types of magazines, radio, television, hard- and soft-cover publishing, comic strips, and finally—newspaper headlines!

But back at the turn of the century, a new medium had flickered into being—the motion picture! Here was an entirely new means of expression, and science-fiction was not long in coming to it.

I. SCIENCE-FICTION IN THE SILENT FILM

It was no accident that one of the first men ever to work in the medium of the motion picture was also the creator of the first science-fiction film. The Frenchman, Georges Méliès, was the man who first saw in the new medium of moving pictures the possibilities of personal expression. His original and imaginative experiments with film started movies on a new course, focusing attention on their creative possibilities and story-telling abilities.

> Méliès discovered magic in the motion picture camera. He turned its lens away from reality—from mere reporting—to fantasy and genuine creation. He also brought to movie making, with his system of "artificially arranged scenes," a conception of organization which was to change the haphazard, improvisational methods of the Americans and fertilize their technique.
>
> . . . .
>
> In 1896 Georges Méliès, thirty-four years old, was a jack-of-all-trades—caricaturist for an anti-Boulangist paper, theatrical producer, actor, scenic painter at the Theatre Houdin, and professional magician. This was the year in which he turned to

moving pictures. From then until the outbreak of the World War he devoted himself to his adopted art.

. . . .

At first Méliès roamed the streets with his camera, "shooting" people, trains, soldiers—anything that moved—for the mere pleasure of it. One day while he was photographing a Paris street scene his camera jammed; the film had caught inside the aperture gate. Méliès cleared the gate, readjusted the film, and resumed shooting. When the film was projected later, he was surprised to see on the screen a bus suddenly turn into a hearse. The bus he had been photographing when the camera jammed had gone its way while he was readjusting the camera, and in its place a hearse had appeared. When Méliès had started shooting again, the camera had taken a picture of the hearse on the same bit of film in the same place where the bus had been photographed.

Being a professional magician, Méliès was greatly excited by the coincidence. He at once visualized the superior "supernatural" capacities of the moving pictures as compared to the ordinary magician. Investigating camera possibilities further, he discovered many more devices for trick effects—effects that were to astound the movie world for many years.[9]

Méliès went into movie making with great enthusiasm and energy, and by 1900 had made over two hundred "magical, mystical and trick films," each only a few minutes in duration. These films were crammed with every conceivable trick effect, and so mystified and startled the audiences that they were immediate successes. They were imported to the United States, where they quickly became the most popular of screen entertainments. Méliès dealt at first solely with the bizarre, the supernatural and the fantastic. His films bore

---

[9]Lewis Jacobs, The Rise of the American Film (New York: Harcourt, Brace and Company, 1939), pp. 22-23.

such titles as : The Vanishing Lady, The Haunted Castle, The Laboratory of Mephistopheles, A Hypnotist at Work, Cagliostro's Mirror, The Bewitched Inn, Conjurer Making 10 Hats in 60 Seconds, and Cinderella.

Then, in 1900, Méliès produced what may technically be called the first science-fiction film ever made. It was called Hydrothérapie fantastique ou le Secret du Docteur (Fantastic Hydrotherapy or The Doctor's Secret), and concerned a doctor (perhaps the screen's first mad scientist!) who had invented a fantastically elaborate hydrotherapy machine. The film's few flickering minutes were crammed with the madcap results of the machine's action on the doctor's first patient. The poor man was literally taken apart and put back together again, much the worse for wear. Although it is doubtful that Méliès had anything so deep in mind, as his films were primarily to entertain, this film could be called the first presentation of the theme of man against the machine. This theme was to dominate a good many science-fiction film makers, down through the decades, as they discovered in prophetic films an excellent vehicle for presenting their anxieties and apprehensions about our increasingly mechanized existence.

Two years later, Méliès turned his attention toward the heavens, and, inspired by the then-popular novels of Jules Verne, produced his most ambitious film to date, the first film to deal with interplanetary travel.

This movie, called A Trip to the Moon (Un Voyage dans la Lune), established him [Méliès] conclusively as the dominant creative imagination in motion pictures. His four-hundredth film, it was 825 feet long, twice the length of Cinderella and at least three times the length of the average movie of the day. It was advertised in his "Star" Catalogue of 1902-1903 as "Ten extraordinary and fantastical cinematographic series in thirty scenes." Certainly it was an eloquent display of his fertile imagination and the graphic possibilities of the motion picture camera for fantasy and satire.

Based on From the Earth to the Moon and Around the Moon, the Jules Verne story, A Trip to the Moon charmingly lampooned the scientific and mechanical interests of the new century. Méliès' experience as a caricaturist enabled him to depict wittily the lunar dream world of the professors and the fantastic hopes of some of the scientific societies. The astronomers who take the journey to the moon are foppish; their preparations are ridiculous. The start from their textbook world with solemn ceremonies, their entry into the moon—right into its eye—and their meeting with the Selenites were nonsense of a high order. Their inglorious return to earth and their reception as heroes—they are crowned and decorated—ends the extravaganza, dispelling the dream atmosphere that has been carefully created.

The scenario for A Trip to the Moon, written by Méliès himself, indicates his order of "artificially arranged scenes," but the bald listing hardly suggests his imaginative intent, the film's rich visual effects, the ingenuity of the camera devices, or the quality of the film's unique style. The scenario follows:

1. The scientific congress at the Astronomic Club.
2. Planning the trip. Appointing the explorers and servants. Farewell.
3. The workshops. Constructing the projectile.
4. The foundries. The chimney-stacks. The casting of the monster gun.
5. The astronomers enter the shell.
6. Loading the gun.
7. The monster gun. March past the gunners. Fire!!! Saluting the flag.
8. The flight through space. Approaching the moon.
9. Landed right in the eye!!!
10. Flight of the shell into the moon. Appearance of the earth from the moon.

11. The plain of craters. Volcanic eruption.
12. The dream (the Solies, the Great Bear, Phoebus, the Twin Sisters, Saturna).
13. The snowstorm.
14. 40 degrees below zero. Descending a lunar crater.
15. Into the interior of the moon. The giant mushroom grotto.
16. Encounter with the Selenites. Homeric flight.
17. Prisoners!!!
18. The kingdom of the moon. The Selenite army.
19. The flight.
20. Wild pursuit.
21. The astronomers find the shell again. Departure from the moon.
22. Vertical drop into space.
23. Splashing into the open sea.
24. At the bottom of the ocean.
25. The rescue. Return to port.
26. The great fête. Triumphal march past.
27. Crowning and decorating the heroes of the trip.
28. Procession of Marines and the Fire Brigade.
29. Inauguration of the commemorative statue by the manager and the council.
30. Public rejoicings.

In every respect _A Trip to the Moon_ towered above the standard production of the day. American pictures, despite two years of competition with Méliès' films, were still absurdly poor. Porter's efforts for the Edison Company were still confined to reproductions of vaudeville skits and scenes of local interest. Blackton of Vitagraph, when not turning out comic-strip novelties, was continuing to make his fake news events; Bitzer and McCutcheon of Biograph were shooting similar subjects. In comparison with such "camera copying," Méliès' films were monumental, quite unmatched for style, ingenuity and imagination.

Some idea of the intricate creative labor that went into _A Trip to the Moon_ can be gathered from a letter Méliès wrote in 1930 to Jean LeRoy, who asked for details:

"I made myself the model sculptured terra cotta and the plaster moldings. . . . The entire cost was about 10,000 francs, a sum relatively high for the time, caused especially by the mechanical sceneries and principally by the cost of the cardboard and canvas costumes made for the Selenites . . . all those articles being made especially and consequently expensive. . . .

"There were not yet stars amongst the artists; their names were never known or written in bills or advertisements. The people employed . . . were entirely acrobats, girls and singers coming from the music halls, the theatrical actors having not yet accepted to play in cinema films, as they considered the motion pictures much below the theatre. They came only later, when they knew that music hall people gained more money in performing films than themselves in playing in theatres. . . . Two years after, my office was, every night, full of theatrical people coming for asking to be engaged. I remember that . . . the Moon (The Woman in the Crescent) was Bleuette Bernon, music hall singer, the Stars were ballet girls, from Théâtre,Du Châtelet—and the men (principal ones) Victor André of the Cluny Théâtre, Delpierre, Farjaux-Kelm-Brunnet, music hall singers, and myself. The Sélenites were acrobats from Folies Bergère."

Not only had Méliès rewritten Jules Verne's story, designed and painted the sets, acted the principal character, directed and organized the film, but he had personally taken care of the business problems. He had hired the cast, designed the costumes, overseen the developing and printing of the film, and financed and sold the production. A prolific and original worker, Méliès was also a precise and forward-looking one.[10]

Méliès continued to produce more "fantastical fantasies," but some trouble with other manufacturers copying or "duping" A Trip to the Moon without regard for its creator's rights led him to employ the device of including a notice of copyright somewhere within one of the scenes in his succeeding films. He still had many imitators, however, such as Secundo de Chomon, a Frenchman who made his own version of a Voyage dans la Lune in 1903, followed by Le Voyage à Jupiter in 1909. Gaston Velle ventured much further afield with his Le Voyage dans une Etoile (The Trip to a Star) in 1906.

---

[10] Ibid., pp. 27-29.

These imitators did not disturb Méliès greatly, because he was still able to outimagine them all, as he conclusively proved in 1904 with his most ambitious and expensive ($7,500) undertaking, _Le Voyage à travers l'Impossible_ (_The Impossible Voyage_).

> This film, like his _Trip to the Moon_, was a satire on scientific societies, but it was far more self-conscious. In forty "motion tableaux" and 1,233 feet of film—Méliès' longest to date—its incredible story told of "The Institute of Incoherent Geography and how they discussed the proposed voyage of a new machine which must surpass in conception and invention all previous expeditions of the learned world." Its farcical intent is apparent not only in the names Méliès gave his savants but in their ludicrous adventures. "Under the Presidency of Professor Polehunter, assisted by Secretary Rattlebrains, and Vice-President Humbug, the Institutes plan a trip of the world."
>
> The conception is in the best Disney fashion, with the scientists poring madly over maps, studying fantastic charts, and examining machines in "Engineer Crazyloff's machine shop." With a great flourish, the learned group finally take off, "employing all the known devices of locomotion—automobiles, dirigibles, balloons, submarines, boats, rockets, etc." And now their adventures begin. "At three hundred miles an hour," they visit the rising sun and the aurora borealis, pass through a solar eruption, get frozen in a heavenly embankment, are thawed out again by an explosion, and eventually land on earth again to receive decorations for their brilliant voyage.
>
> This film expressed all of Méliès' talents. In it his feeling for caricature, painting, theatrical invention, and camera science became triumphant. The complexity of his tricks, his resourcefulness with mechanical contrivances, the imaginativeness of the settings, and the sumptuous tableaux made the film a masterpiece for its day.[11]

Turning from planets and galaxies, Méliès once again paraphrased Jules Verne and produced _Deux cent mille lieues sous les mers_

---

[11] _Ibid._, pp. 30-31.

ou Le Cauchemar d'un Pecheur (20,000 Leagues Under the Seas or A Fisherman's Nightmare) in 1907. Here Méliès had a whole new world to design and create, and he produced an astounding and ornate undersea world, complete with mermaids and sea monsters. That same year, he tried another short project called Le Tunnel sous la Manche ou Le Cauchemar Franco-anglais (The Tunnel Under the English Channel or the Franco-English Nightmare).

After 1907, Méliès' popularity began to wane, under the press of new techniques, new men and new ideas, until finally he dropped from sight almost entirely. On January 22, 1938 he died in France, penniless, his grim decline in merciless contrast to the light-hearted, rollicking fantasies he made for the world.

His lessons were not forgotten, for other film makers turned to scientific and prophetic themes for screen entertainment. The airplane was a fascinating subject for speculation in the early 1900's, and the first American-made science-fiction film dealt with an advance-designed Airship (Vitagraph, 1908). France also showed an interest in prophetic aircraft, with Latest Style Airship (1908). The Battle in the Clouds (Urban, 1910) was an amusing farce about an imaginary sky battle between men in balloon-type aircraft, and Thomas Edison decided to visit the heavens in A Trip to Mars (1910). Other prophetic films of the times included one from Italy, called If One Could See the Future (1911); The Times Are Out of Joint (France, 1910), and A Strike in the

Make-Young Business (France, 1911), the first screen treatment of the theme of rejuvenation.

France had been the leader in the science-fiction film, but after the beginning of World War I, there was a decline in film-making there, and foreign films were beginning to invade the markets.

> During this early period of crisis—when the war had caused a considerable reduction in film-making, and also turned audiences against the hitherto popular sadistic melodramas—the first avant-garde film appeared.
>
> This was Abel Gance's La Folie du Docteur Tube [The Madness of Dr. Tube] (1914), in which a madman succeeded in breaking up light rays by an ingenious system of crystal tubes, creating thereby a cinematic world of deformity five years before the advent of Dr. Caligari. Gance's expressionistic use of distorting lenses, mirrors and out-of-focus photography proved too great a shock to his producers, however, and the film was not released.[12]

Serials have proved to be a prolific source of science-fiction down through the years although it is usually employed only as a background or framework for action-packed adventures, rather than as a serious theme. The first serial utilizing elements of science-fiction was called Diamond in the Sky, made in 1915.

The year 1916 was a bountiful one for science-fiction. D. W. Griffith became interested in the filmic possibilities of prophecy, and wrote and produced a box-office hit called The Flying Torpedo.

> Directed by Jack O'Brien, featuring John Emerson and Bessie Love, this was a prophetic vision of the invasion of Southern

---

[12]Peter John Dyer, "Some Personal Visions," Films and Filming, November, 1958, p. 13.

California by an Asiatic horde in flying torpedos, using robot bombs as weapons![13]

> . . . an eccentric detective story-writer . . . [thwarts] an imaginary invasion of the U. S. in 1921 by the invention of a radio-controlled aerial torpedo. . . . The photography was by George Hill, later a director, and the "torpedo" was devised by the McCarthy brothers, afterwards well known for their special effects.[14]

Film makers in 1916 seemed preoccupied with grim subjects, for in the U. S. Great Northern produced *The End of the World* and Vitagraph made *The Last Man*. Perhaps these films were the result of war jitters, for in France:

> Undeterred, Gance experimented with Science Fiction in *Le Gaz Mortel* [*The Deadly Gas*] (1916), and for the next twenty-odd years, continued to try the patience of all but the most ardent *cinéastes* with incredible super-films on an heroic, Victor Hugo scale, that had one supreme vice—an utter inability to be simple.[15]

In Germany, the "other side" made some films in a somewhat lighter vein of science-fiction. Otto Ripert directed a serial called *Homunkulus, Der Führer* (*Homunculus, the Leader*), in which Olaf Fenns played the part of the screen's first artificially created man, the ancestor of the robots and the Frankenstein Monster to come. This film was probably used for propaganda purposes, to help promote the

---

[13] Peter John Dyer, "Some Nights of Horror," *Films and Filming*, June, 1958, p. 13.

[14] Harold Dunham, "Bessie Love," *Films in Review*, February, 1959, p. 87.

[15] Dyer, "Some Personal Visions," *loc. cit.*

concept of the "Master Race" in Germany,[16] just as Die Grosse Wette (The Great Bet) was intended to ridicule the "decadent American capitalists." This last was a fascinating film, however, and showed great ingenuity and inventiveness. The Moving Picture World took note of it:

> An extraordinary film which is at present causing much comment is Harry Piel's newest work, Die Grosse Wette (The Great Bet), which is having its premier at the Marmohaus. The action of this film is supposed to take place in the year 2,000 and Mr. Piel has endeavored to give a representation of the world as it will be at that period. Needless to say, astonishing and technical tricks, including an airline cab-service, an exceedingly cleverly constructed millionaire's palace with all twenty-first century conveniences, a library whose books step out of place by merely pressing upon a button, were used as means toward showing life in the next century. An interesting plot revolving about an American millionaire who bets his fortune upon his ability to live three days with a tricky automatic figure forms the substance of the story throughout which many interesting things happen. Criticisms over the film are divided, but in general the work has been favorably received, inasmuch as it is a change from the ordinary love drama and also points the way toward a new school in films. The leading parts lie in the hands of Mizzi Wirth and Ludwig Hartmann, who executed their respective roles with great understanding. Especially commendable are the settings which Mr. Piel has arranged for this film.[17]

J. E. Williamson decided to film Jules Verne's classic, Twenty Thousand Leagues Under the Sea, in 1916, treating the story much

---

[16]For more information on the effects of German feelings as mirrored in their films, see Siegfried Kracauer, From Caligari to Hitler (Princeton, New Jersey: Princeton University Press, 1947), pp. 31-33.

[17]"German Trade Notes," The Moving Picture World, April 1, 1916, p. 71.

more realistically and faithfully than had Méliès in 1907. This film was fast-paced and fascinating, with many interesting special effects, and "was probably the first feature production to utilize under-water photography. . . ."[18]

> . . . in 1915 he [Williamson] embarked on a film version of Jules Verne's Twenty Thousand Leagues Under the Sea. He spared no pains in the interests of realism, even constructing a dummy octopus of imposing dimensions with coiled spring and india-rubber arms, worked by a man crouching inside its body. Once more fortune smiled on the financial results of submarine photography, even going so far as to arrange that the German U-boat which popped up so dramatically in New York at this stage of the War, thereby focussing men's minds on subaqueous affairs, should do so on the very day of the film's opening show.[19]

In 1918 Denmark produced what Michel Laclos calls the "first true science fiction film,"[20] Himmelskibet (The Sky Ship), directed by Holger-Madsen.

> In 1918, Ole Olson himself, the former market exhibitor who by the force of his bold illiteracy had been able to see the possibilities of a new art medium, got over-literary and wrote the script of The Sky Ship (or Heaven Ship, whichever you prefer). It described how a group of young idealists set out in a rocket for Mars and found the inhabitants there very noble, clad in white robes, waving palm leaves in honor of peace. They took the prettiest Mars girl with them back to the earth in order that she might persuade the

---

[18] Richard Kraft, "Book Reviews," Films in Review, August-September, 1957, p. 359.

[19] H. D. Waley, "Book Reviews," Sight and Sound, Spring, 1936, p. 43.

[20] Michel Laclos, Le Fantastique au Cinéma (Paris: Jean-Jacques Pauvert, 1958), p. xxix.

earthdwellers to stop World War I![21]

That same year saw the production of _Loutch Smerti_ (_The Death Ray_) in Russia by Lev Kuleshov. The screenplay for this film was by no less a figure than Pudovkin!

The year 1920 brought two films of interest, Tower Films' _Trip to Mars_ and another Russian picture, produced by Mezhrabpom-Russ, and directed by Protazanov. Based on a play by Count Alexei Tolstoy, _Aelita_ presented "on a cubist Mars, a _Metropolis_-like society in the throes of savage class-war."[22]

> . . . the big decorative production of _Aelita_ . . . was an extraordinary Martian fantasy, combining the events in Russia during 1917 and 1918 with a fictitious story on the planet; it was notable for its wonderful massed grouping of crowds and for the cubist settings and costumes designed by Isaac Rabinovitch and Madame Alexandra Exter, of the Kamerny Theatre, Moscow.[23]

The world ended again in 1921, a subject which was to be treated many times hence, and in many different ways. Paramount produced _At the End of the World_, and Metro received a _Message from Mars_. The following year a man named George Folsey found himself fascinated

---

[21] Ebbe Neergaard, "The Rise, the Fall, and the Rise of Danish Film," _Hollywood Quarterly_, Spring, 1950, pp. 220-221.

[22] Dyer, _op. cit._, p. 31.

[23] Paul Rotha, _The Film Till Now_ (London: Jonathan Cape, 1930), pp. 154-155.

by the Red Planet also, and photographed the first science-fiction film in 3-D! Crude as it was, The Man from Mars featured unearthly creatures with huge heads and gleaming talons and was quite a shocker in its day. Paramount tried a tale of prescience this year, with The Man Who Saw Tomorrow (1922).

The following year, in France, two interesting films were produced. The first was directed by none other than René Clair, and starred Henri Rollan, Albert Prejean and Madeline Rodriques. It was a farce concerning an invisible ray which made people do crazy things while they were asleep. It was called Paris qui dort or Le Rayon Invisible (Paris Asleep or The Invisible Ray) (1923). To avoid confusion with a later film, it has also been listed as The Crazy Ray, perhaps a more apt title. The second film was directed by the famed French silent film director, Marcel L'Herbier, to whom Peter John Dyer refers as "a literary aesthete in the Oscar Wilde manner."[24]

> L'Inhumaine [The Living Dead Man] (1923) is interesting, not for L'Herbier's typically remote, frigid direction, but in its curious story and brilliant art direction. Eve Francis, her tragedienne's face working hard to inject some life into L'Herbier's abstractions, played a singer who treats all her lovers badly until, poisoned by a jealous Maharajah, she is saved by an engineer's dangerous laboratory experiment. The sets, designed in the cubist style by Leger and Robert Mallet-Stevens, and their assistants, Claude Autant-Lara and Alberto Cavalcanti, had a marked influence on Fritz Lang's Metropolis three years later.[25]

In addition to all the talent gathered together on the art direction of this

---

[24]Dyer, op. cit., p. 14. [25]Ibid., pp. 14-15.

film, L'Inhumaine also had a score composed especially for it by Darius Milhaud.

The year 1924 brought us back to that ever-popular subject once again, Allied Producers and Distributors made The End of the World, and Fox produced The Last Man on Earth, starring Earle Foxe and Grace Canard, in which a strange disease killed off all the world's male population—save one!

Advanced aircraft flashed through the air in 1925 in Air Hawks (Film Booking Office), and Sir Arthur Conan Doyle's thrilling novel of a prehistoric land was brought to the screen by First National, directed by Harry G. Hoyt. The Lost World told of an expedition to a plateau forgotten by time, deep in the African jungle. Wallace Beery, as Doyle's crusty old explorer, Professor Challenger, led the party (consisting of Lewis Stone, Bessie Love and Lloyd Hughes) in and out of many hair-raising adventures, including encounters with giant dinosaurs and sub-human ape men. Finally a brontosaurus is disabled and falls off the plateau. The adventurers devise a method of moving him and take him back to London to be exhibited. However, once there, he breaks loose and causes considerable havoc before swimming down the Thames and out to sea. This film was a landmark in special effects, and the dinosaurs were as convincing as any have been since. They were the work of Fred Jackman and Willis O'Brien, who was to become famous later with his trick work in King Kong.

A borderline science-fiction film was made in Germany the following year by UFA, called

> . . . Am Rande der Welt (At the Edge of the World), a passionate appeal for world peace written and directed by Karl Grune, with Brigitte Helm playing the female lead.[26]

This film was notable for its design, by A. D. Neppach, and for the fact that it starred young Wilhelm (William) Dieterle.

But this film was overshadowed by another UFA production of 1926, a giant of a film destined to stand as one of the landmarks of the science-fiction film. Fritz Lang's Metropolis, based on a novel by his wife, Thea von Harbou, touched off a great deal of controversy. Paul Rotha defended it:

> Of Metropolis, more wilful abuse has been written than praise, partly because the version shown in this country [England] was unhappily edited, many sequences being deliberately removed. The English copy was arranged by Channing Pollock, author of The Fool. The film, when it made its London appearance, was not enthusiastically received. H. G. Wells, amongst others, damned it as "quite the silliest film. . . ." As a matter of fact, Metropolis was very remarkable, based on a brilliant filmic conception, and, had it been shown in its entirety, would have afforded a wonderful exposition of cinematography. As with all of the German studio-films, the binding keynote of the picture was its amazing architecture. It is not until we compare Metropolis with a British picture on the same lines, Maurice Elvey's High Treason, that it is possible to realise its value. There is not one member of the production units or executive committees; not one critic or film journalist in this country, who can afford to sneer at Fritz Lang's conception. High Treason, with its arts-and-crafts design by Andrew Mazzei, revealed only too clearly how poorly England produces a film of this kind. Though neither a great film nor an example of pure

---

[26] Herbert G. Luft, "William Dieterle," Films in Review, April, 1957, p. 151.

> filmic expression, Metropolis contained scenes that for their grandeur and strength have never been equalled either by England or America. Who, for example, could have handled the sequence when Rotwang transfers life and the likeness of human form into the steel figure with such brilliant feeling as Fritz Lang? Metropolis, with its rows of rectangular windows, its slow-treading workers, its great geometric buildings, its contrasted light and shade, its massed masses, its machinery, was a considerable achievement. Its actual story value was negligible; the architecture was the story in itself.[27]

Peter John Dyer looked deeper into the meaning of the film:

> . . . Lang's Metropolis [is] . . . a prophetic vision of a machine-over-man city worked by slaves, imprisoned in a labyrinthine underworld at the mercy of an insane, tyrannical scientist (Rudolph Klein-Rogge). In its expert showmanship, fertile imagination, technical perfection and creation of a new world of unbearable, terrifying vitality, Metropolis remained unrivalled until Orphée. Its "Orpheus" descending into the underworld is the traditional blonde in knickerbockers, over-emotional and consumed with love —played here by Gustav Frohlich. Its "Eurydice" is Maria, "a simple girl of the people," played here by Brigitte Helm. . . . Like Orphée, in fact, Metropolis is rich in fascinating subconscious content that has passed through the mirror of consciousness without being questioned.[28]

Metropolis was the first film to portray convincingly a world of the future on the screen. The futuristic buildings, inventions and machines were marvelous to behold, and the film introduced the screen's first robot—a fascinating female one, played by Brigitte Helm. The sequence of her creation is pure science-fiction magic, and has yet to be matched for sheer power in any science-fiction or horror film, including Frankenstein. But there were those who were not so enthusiastic, as typified by John Grierson:

---

[27]Rotha, op. cit., pp. 193-194. [28]Dyer, op. cit., p. 31.

> Metropolis, for all its pretension of setting and high-flying issue between capital and labour, concluded sillily and sentimentally that "it was love that made the world go round." As H. G. Wells pointed out at the time, it was an infant conception, without knowledge of society or science. Lang, I think, only ever peeps into the great problems. Looking into the hinterlands of space and time and the mind itself—in The Girl in the Moon, in Metropolis, in Mabuse, and in M he is satisfied in the end with the honours of melodrama.[29]

Another artificial being came into existence in 1928, an "Android" or artificial human, similar to Homunculus. This being was a woman, and proved so popular with the German people that the film was remade twice afterwards. Again, the feelings of frustration and inferiority of an abnormal creature touched a responsive chord in the German psyche.[30] Produced by UFA and directed by Henrik Galeen,

> . . . Alraune (Unholy Love, 1928) . . . was based upon a novel by H. H. Ewers. A scientist (Paul Wegener), experimenting in artificial insemination, creates a human being: Alraune, daughter of a hanged criminal and a prostitute. This creature, portrayed by Brigitte Helm as a somnambulant vamp with seductive and empty features, ruins all those who are in love with her, and at the end destroys herself. Alraune's family resemblance to Homunculus is apparent. In her case, too, abnormal origins are called upon to account for inner frustration and its devastating consequences.[31]

Hollywood recalled the success of Universal's Twenty Thousand Leagues Under the Sea back in 1916. In 1925, J. E. Williamson came

---

[29] John Grierson, "Directors of the 'Thirties," Grierson on Documentary, Forsyth Hardy, editor (Longon and Glasgow: Collins, 1946), p. 45.

[30] Siegfried Kracauer, From Caligari to Hitler (Princeton, New Jersey: Princeton University Press, 1947), pp. 153-154.

[31] Ibid.

to Hollywood to plan a sequel, the one Jules Verne himself wrote, The Mysterious Island.

> Needless to say, Hollywood envisaged not a sequel merely but a super-sequel. The players were to be stars, the photographs were to be in colour. Waves of hectic activity swept over the scenario department. The scene was to be in America, the scene was to be in Russia, the scene was to be nowhere in particular. . . . finally, however, the film got made, only to be blighted at birth by the advent of the talkies.[32]

This film was the first science-fiction picture to utilize color and sound, two elements which were to open up new worlds of endeavor for the portrayal of science-fiction on the screen.

> MGM's The Mysterious Island, made in 1929 by Maurice Tourneur, that French specialist of the macabre, was a definite portent of the future in that it used sound to increase the melodramatic thrills of its science-fiction scenes.[33]

Despite its ambition, the film was not much of a success with the critics:

> Jules Verne's scientific romance in which he predicts the submarine and speculated about a half-human race living at tremendous depths on the floor of the ocean, has not come out so well. As the old inventor of the submarine, Lionel Barrymore does a great deal of leering and wig-shaking, and in a few short talking sequences he covers his face with his hand.
>
> We who go to the movies do not expect scientific accuracy in an adventure story, but the technical absurdities in The Mysterious Island will be obvious to anyone who has had even the slight

---

[32] H. D. Waley, "Book Reviews," Sight and Sound, Spring, 1956, pp. 43-44.

[33] William K. Everson, "Horror Films," Films in Review, January, 1954, p. 20.

experience gained from running a toy train. It seems that old Dr. Barrymore, assisted by an arty looking crowd of "mechanics" dressed in Russian smocks, has built a submarine. His sister, permanently attired in an evening dress, wanders here and there in the machine shop. Pretty soon there is a revolution and everybody goes diving about in lovely cardboard submarines full of wheels and levers and flashing signal lights.

The most interesting sequences are those showing a gigantic octopus leading a swarm of tiny under-sea men to battle against the submarines.

Jules Verne may not have been accurate in every detail, but he always built up his stories so that they sounded possible. The Mysterious Island is even less possible than Little Nemo used to be. Due to faulty technicoloring all the characters are rather violently red in the face.

An interesting technical point arises when the hero and heroine, both securely wrapped in heavy steel diving suits, meet at the bottom of the ocean, and float toward each other. A clinch is in order but, for once, absurdly impossible. The old routine is broken and the audience is so pleased that it laughs aloud.[34]

As the era of the silent film drew to a close, Fritz Lang returned to science-fiction with his Frau im Mond (The Girl in the Moon), in which he

> . . . imagined a rocket projectile carrying passengers to the moon. The cosmic enterprise was staged with a surprising veracity of vision; the plot was pitiable for its emotional shortcomings. These were so obvious that they discredited many an illusion Lang tried to create by showy virtuosity. The lunar landscape smelled distinctly of UFA's Neubabelsberg studios.[35]

This film featured a rocket ship designed by the noted German rocket

---

[34]Creighton Peet, "The Movies," Outlook, January 1, 1930, p. 33.

[35]Kracauer, op. cit., p. 151.

expert, Dr. Hermann Oberth, and Walt Disney included a portion of it in his 1955 documentary, *Man in Space*. Peter John Dyer, in the British magazine *Films and Filming*, summed up some of the shortcomings of the science-fiction film, as it had progressed over the first thirty years of the cinema, from the first flickering moon-bullet of Georges Méliès to the flaming space ship of Fritz Lang's lunar voyage:

> If these films, . . . have failed in persuading us to accept a vision of any other world than our own, it is because their science-fiction remains schizophrenic. Part monster-horror film, part mechanical fantasy, they somehow never contrive to insert that necessary, authentic strangeness between two *real* worlds which would throw them both into relief, and so reveal a supernatural vision.[36]

II. FROM 1930 TO 1949

The Depression years gave birth to a great many films designed to make the audiences forget the hardships of the times. Lavish musicals, zany comedies, extravagant historical pageants, this cinematic Lethe poured out of Hollywood—and the people responded hungrily. Producers found in the medium of science-fiction an excellent vehicle for escape, as such lavish films as *Just Imagine* proved. Directed by David Butler, *Just Imagine* offered music and songs by Henderson, DeSylva and Brown and starred El Brendel and Maureen O'Sullivan.

---

[36] Dyer, *loc. cit.*

> An . . . interesting future spectacle . . . that would bear revival, is David Butler's Just Imagine, made for Fox in 1930. It contained a fascinating conception of what New York *might* look like in 1980, and its sets of the ultra-streamlined metropolis of the future are imaginative *and* realistic. The "aerial automobiles," which, it is claimed, will provide regular transit service, are not too far removed from helicopters. Unfortunately, Just Imagine spent too much time with the comicalities of its star (El Brendel) and not enough with fantasy. Some of its spectacular shots of the future New York were later incorporated in the Universal serial Buck Rogers, which can now be seen on television.[37]

But the audiences loved it. Some idea of the type of thing that went on can be gained from the following account by Forrest J Ackerman:

> [Just Imagine was] . . . a memorable musicomedy of a flight to Mars in 1980. . . . In the latter, J-21 and LN-18, a boy and girl of 1980, were showing Single-O, a survivor from 1930 who had been unconscious for 50 years, the technological advances of their scientific era. Inserting a coin in a device that looked like a combination between a jukebox and a pinball machine, they pressed a button and a couple of pills popped out. One, they explained to him, was steak, the other apple pie. After he had swallowed both, they asked him how he had enjoyed his meal. "The steak was a little tough," he reported ruefully. "Give me the good old days." Another button was pressed, another miracle of speed and compaction wrought before the eyes of the visitor from the past, who only shook his head and repeated, "Give me the good old days." Finally, the couple demonstrated the modern method of producing children. Preselecting the infant's sex, they pulled a lever and down a slide slid a freshly-diapered brand-new "bundle of joy." The man from the past looked aghast and with a newfound and heartfelt expression said for the third time what he had said originally: "*Give me the good old days!*" This was daring and risqué dialogue a quarter of a century ago, and it fractured audiences.[38]

---

[37] William K. Everson, "Film Spectacles," Films in Review, November, 1954, p. 470.

[38] Forrest J Ackerman, "Confessions of a Science Fiction Addict," After Hours, 1:4, 1957, pp. 10-11. MGM also produced a short subject that year, called The Spirit of 1976, having to do with future patriotism.

This film was the first science-fiction talkie made in America. In Britain, the first all-talking picture was a forecast of life in 1940, Maurice Elvey's High Treason. Made along the same lines as Metropolis and Just Imagine, it attempted to forecast the future, but lacked the imagination of the other two films.[39] Some of its prophetic inventions were interesting, such as the "telephotophone," which allowed two people to see each other while conversing. Its female star was Benita Hume, who later married Ronald Colman.

In Germany, 1930 saw a re-make in sound of Alraune, directed by Richard Oswald and again starring Brigitte Helm as the artificially created femme fatale. In 1931, a German film called Der Tunnel (The Tunnel) was made, based on a novel by Bernhard Kellermann, which concerned an attempt at building an underwater tunnel beneath the Atlantic Ocean. In France, Abel Gance turned out another of his over-long epics entitled La Fin du Monde (The End of the World). As with his other films, this one was "vast and vaguely ideological . . . haunted by the symbolic image of 'The Spirit of France,' and . . . verging on Science Fiction."[40]

William Dieterle directed a semi-scientific drama in 1932 called Six Hours to Live, starring Warner Baxter and released by Fox. But what little position the legitimate science-fiction film did have in

---

[39] Supra, p. 33. [40] Dyer, op. cit., p. 13.

he Industry was usurped in 1931 by the advent and immediate success f Frankenstein and Dracula. Boris Karloff and Bela Lugosi became he kings of horror, and a landslide of horror films began coming out f Hollywood. Such films as Dr. X, The Old Dark House, The Island f Lost Souls[41] and Dr. Jekyll and Mr. Hyde (with Frederic March) oncentrated on the supernatural and the macabre, with only a few ather poor films retaining even a few elements of science-fiction. ;ven then, these were usually subordinate to the horror elements.)ne such film was Chandu the Magician (Fox, 1932).

> Chandu (The Magician) (1932) came at the end of 1932, climaxing a year of malodorous horror efforts. As Chandu, Edmund Lowe is shouldered with the terrible responsibility of saving the world from the demented Bela Lugosi, who has stolen a powerful electric ray and is determined to toast civilization to a crisp. Adapted from a top-ranking radio serial, Chandu carried its pointless story to the edge of human reason, garnering more guffaws than gasps.
>
> The cinema's use of super-science for thriller purposes spins dizzily off the planet and puts more things in heaven and earth than were ever dreamed in anybody's philosophy.[42]

'here were two sequels made, in the form of serials, in the following

---

[41] This film deserves mention briefly, because although pri- ıarily a horror film in approach, it was based on H. G. Wells' novel, 'he Island of Dr. Moreau. Charles Laughton played the diabolical Dr. Ioreau, who surgically transformed men into animals. Bela Lugosi layed the leader of the animal-men in the film, a kind of 'scientifically created werewolf."

[42] Jack Nealon, "An Historical and Critical Survey of the .merican Horror Film Since 1930" (unpublished Master's thesis, The 'niversity of Southern California, Los Angeles, 1953), p. 95.

years. Neither of these, however, contained any super-scientific or science-fictional elements, but would more logically be classed as fantasies. Bela Lugosi starred in both Return of Chandu (1934) and Chandu on the Magic Island (1935).

The year 1933 saw the production of a great many "borderline cases" of science-fiction, such as Fox's Berkeley Square, which was actually a historical picture, although it contained elements of time travel. Based on the play by John L. Balderston and John Collins Squire, Leslie Howard played the part of a man projected back in time to the 18th century, where he met and fell in love with Heather Angel. It was not a particular success, as Paul Rotha notes:

> The romantic school is again well-represented in the Fox Berkeley Square, a delicate piece of staging that carries good acting by Leslie Howard, and has not received all the plaudits it deserves. . . . Its attraction lies in two features not usually found in Hollywood productions: first, emotional delicacy and sincerity; second, historical setting that carries conviction both in atmosphere and in detail.[43]

That same year (1933), RKO produced a true science-fiction spectacle of earth's inundation by a second great flood, based on the novel by S. Fowler Wright. Deluge starred Sidney Blackmer and Peggy Shannon, and contained some magnificent scenes of destruction

---

[43]Paul Rotha, "Films of the Quarter," Sight and Sound, Winter 1933-34, p. 142. When Berkeley Square was re-made in 1951 as I'll Never Forget You, the science-fiction aspect was strengthened by having the time-shift caused by an atomic experiment gone wrong. Cf. post, p. 87.

by special effects man Ned Mann, who was later to prove himself as one of the best in the field. Some of these scenes were later incorporated in a film called S. O. S. Tidal Wave and at least one cheap serial.[44] In Germany, UFA produced a film containing an interesting and advanced scientific concept, F. P. 1, or Floating Platform No. 1 (1933). Based on the novel F. P. 1 Antwortet Nicht (F. P. 1 Does Not Answer), by Kurt (later Curt) Siodmak, it was directed by Karl Hartl and released in four different versions in the same year: the German version starred Hans Albers, Paul Hartmann and Sybille Schmitz; a British version, released by Fox Gaumont, starred Leslie Fenton and Conrad Veidt; a French version starred Charles Boyer, and a Spanish version was also released.[45] Kurt Siodmak's story of marvelous floating cities was only the first in a long series of ingenious ideas and screenplays which he was destined to bring to the world of the science-fiction film.

Meanwhile, in Hollywood, James Whale, one of Universal's fair-haired directors, who had proven himself by directing the smash success, Frankenstein, for Carl Laemmle, Jr.—and later, The Old Dark House—was looking around for good story material for another horror film. He found what he was looking for in a novel by H. G.

---

[44] Forrest J. Ackerman, "Letters," It, Winter, 1956, p. 76.

[45] Ibid.

Wells, The Invisible Man. His approach to this story was primarily as a tale of horror, and indeed the Invisible Man does become horrible under the weight of his affliction, but the "gimmick" was primarily a science-fiction one.

> The Invisible Man, it is true, bears some family resemblance to the Frankenstein films, since the Invisible Man himself (Claude Rains) is a figure whose mythical possibilities, though latent and undeveloped, seem potentially as rich as those of the Monster.
>
> The Man has invented a drug with which, in its experimental stages "a dog was injected and turned white like a statue." In its final form the drug gives invisibility; and the Man, having taken it, seeks refuge in a village while he tries to discover an antidote. He succumbs to megalomania, forces his ex-colleague to help him, and sets out to terrorize the world into capitulation. Murders, the wrecking of a train, mental demoralisation, are his weapons. But he is traced to a hay-filled barn in a snow-covered countryside and the police set fire to his refuge. The smoke wakes him and drowsily he flings himself from the barn; his footprints appear in the snow, the police shoot at the space above and the snow is disturbed when he falls. Only when he dies in the hospital does he "return" physically.
>
> Whale's offbeat humor reappears in this film: the policemen are not stupid, but, although they win in the end, all their moves seem pathetically ineffectual as the Man hurtles amongst them, flinging gibes from the invisible pedestal of his would-be godhead. And this grotesque humor goes hand in hand with a sort of hypnotic magic. The tricks necessitated by the Man's invisibility are brilliantly managed and, except on a few rare occasions, completely integrated: a bandaged head wearing dark glasses appears; gloved hands come up and unwind the first layer of bandages; those underneath fit the face and look like a soft, bleached and broken skull. These, in turn, are unwound from the globe of an invisible head. . . . Nothingness rebandages itself, replaces the dark glasses, puts on a silk dressing-gown and hierarchically stalks away.[46]

---

[46]Roy Edwards, "Movie Gothick: A Tribute to James Whale," Sight and Sound, Autumn, 1957, pp. 97-98.

> Whale's . . . venture . . . [was] into the super-human realm. . . . Strong in plot and atmosphere, masterly in its trick photography, this power fantasy, for all its offbeat humor, is the nearest Whale ever got to the German tradition of Paul Wegener. Of several inferior sequels, the first—The Invisible Man Returns (1940, Vincent Price and Cedric Hardwicke)—had both a German screenwriter, Curt Siodmak, and director, Joe May.[47]

The 1933 Invisible Man introduced Claude Rains to the screen, although he only appeared visibly in the last few moments of the film, and gave a "skillful, convincing interpretation of that kind of lunatic hopelessness so often attempted and so seldom attained on American horror screens. The film proper was a modest classic of cinematic magic."[48]

The greatest spectacle to come out of the year 1933 was the mighty King Kong, probably the most popular fantasy film ever made. Produced and directed by Ernest B. Schoedsack and Merian C. Cooper, written by Edgar Wallace and Merian C. Cooper, and starring Fay Wray, Robert Armstrong and Bruce Cabot, this film has been re-released over and over again since 1933, and has appeared repeatedly on television. Executive producer was David O. Selznick, and Willis O'Brien created some of the most spectacular special effects ever

---

[47] Peter John Dyer, "Some Nights of Horror," op. cit., p. 34. Other films of invisibility followed the 1940 sequel, such as The Invisible Woman (1941); The Invisible Agent (1942), with Ilona Massey and Peter Lorre; The Invisible Man's Revenge (1944), and finally Abbott and Costello Meet the Invisible Man (1951). None of these films reached the standards of the original, and none dealt with the original characters, yet several claimed to be "based on the story by H. G. Wells."

[48] Nealon, op. cit., p. 88.

seen on film. King Kong proved to be the financial darling of RKO, and saved that studio from bankruptcy in the 'thirties.[49] This film is actually more of a fantasy than science-fiction. The reason for the ape's immense size and the lack of evolution on Kong Island, producing prehistoric dinosaurs, is never satisfactorily explained. Had it been brought out that, say, radiation of some sort had caused these fantastic effects, as in many later films featuring giant creatures, King Kong could be classed easily as science-fiction. No matter how wild the results, they would at least have been based on scientific speculation. But no matter; as Jack Nealon so aptly states in his thesis on the horror film, "When all is said and done, King Kong is colossal enough to warrant copy in almost all film histories."[50] Basically, what happens in the film is this:

> King Kong is the story of an independent producer's (Robert Armstrong) ambition to give the american film public a wonderfully different kind of adventure movie. He gets an unemployed and starving ex-film actress (Fay Wray), a production crew, and all the necessary paraphernalia his tight budget will allow, and departs for an uncharted island in the South Seas. When Fay Wray is kidnapped by a tribe of black Kong worshippers and laced to a huge post to be sacrificed to the god, Kong, Armstrong and his men raid the tribal community, unlease havoc, but fail to save the screeching captive from the monster. So they pursue them deep into the treacherous, prehistoric jungle. The further in they go, the fewer their numbers become: some of the crew is shaken off a suspension bridge and topple down into a ravine, others drown

---

[49] "Cinema," Time, July 14, 1952, p. 92.

[50] Nealon, op. cit., p. 150.

when their raft is capsized by a water reptile. The survivors are no luckier: they have to tolerate the bothersome intrusions of snakes, giant lizards, reptilic birds, and brontosauri, without so much as a rifle to fend them off. When Kong is eventually cornered, the crew bombards him with anesthesia-like grenades and his carcass is borne to New York, where he is advertised as the "seventh wonder of the world." During a premiere at which the unhappy Kong is the attraction, the monster snaps his iron manacles, escapes the theater amid waves of audience consternation, wrecks an elevated subway, scales a sky-scraper to kidnap Fay Wray in her hotel room, and then proceeds to the tower of the Empire State Building to show off his captive fiancée to the reeling metropolis below. New York sends out a squadron of fighter planes to oust the beast from his eyrie. Kong squashes one or two planes for good measure before admitting defeat and tumbling downward a hundred and one stories. Fay Wray, miraculously rescued, nervously relates her experiences to a cordon of question-tossing reporters.[51]

> . . . Where the film is really good is in the skill with which the monster has been made to work. There is a magnificently contrived fight between Kong and a megalosaurus. The scenery, too, is extremely well contrived, and I should imagine that the animal noises were recorded in some amenable zoo. Technically, the double photography is excellent, and my only criticism of the whole film is that not at any moment is the note of terror struck. It is all just very good fun, and my view is that [Edgar] Wallace had a first-class idea and that Hollywood spoiled it by biting off more than a brontosaurus could chew. Indeed at moments intended to be horrific, I heard more than a suspicion of laughter. If, however, the film fails as a provoker of sheer, unalloyed terror, it succeeds as an extravagant bit of entertainment. . . . It's certain that nobody can be bored.[52]

If the producers did not intend for this film to be taken with complete seriousness, even less did they intend this for the sequel they

---

[51] Ibid., pp. 151-153.

[52] James Agate, Around Cinemas, Vol. II (Amsterdam, Holland: Home and Van Thal Ltd., 1948), pp. 89-90.

made the same year, The Son of Kong. The same directors, writers, crew and much of the same cast were involved, as the explorers returned to Kong Island, looking for another specimen. They encountered more dinosaurs and found a "baby" Kong, about half the size of his papa, but still as big as a house. This little ape was more playful than menacing, and at the end of the farce, he saved the life of the explorer by sacrificing his own when the entire island sank into the sea. Again the special effects were excellent, but the plot seemed to be designed more as a lampoon on King Kong than anything else.

Two final films from the prolific year of 1933 were MGM's Men Must Fight, starring Diana Wynyard, and Fox's It's Great to be Alive, directed by Alfred Worker and starring Paul Roulien and Gloria Stuart. The latter was a musical-comedy re-make of The Last Man on Earth (1924), and had

> . . . the world's sole male survivor of the man-destroying masculitis being a premium priority piece of beefcake on the female market. The most beautiful women in all the world came before Mr. Lucky, as slaves before a Sultan, to bid for his favor.[53]

The year 1934 saw the production in Germany of a film entitled simply Gold, in which "Serge de Poligny revived the tradition of alchemy and attempted to make gold by smashing atoms of lead."[54]

---

[53]Ackerman, "Confessions of a Science-Fiction Addict," op. cit., p. 11.

[54]Michel Laclos, op. cit., p. xxx.

William K. Everson, in Films in Review, called it "an unremarkable and rather turgid film except for wonderfully spectacular 'atom-smashing' footage."[55] So spectacular was this footage, apparently, that it was later used in the climactic scenes of The Magnetic Monster (1953). Despite the fact that this film was made almost twenty years later, "the different footages were very neatly matched up—even to Richard Carlson donning out-of-date overalls and cap, so that, in close-up, he would resemble Hans Albers in long-shot!"[56] Birth of a Robot was an experimental color short subject produced in Britain in 1934 by Charles H. Dand, directed by Humphrey Jennings.

In 1935 the famous Russian director Alexander Dovzhenko wrote and directed a futuristic allegory called Aerograd (Air City), and Columbia Pictures produced Air Hawks, a remake of the earlier 1925 version. Invincible made Death from a Distance, and Universal released Life Returns, about a doctor tampering with the secret of life. The Phantom Empire (Mascot, 1935) was a serial in which even Gene Autry ventured cautiously into the world of science fiction. This serial, starring Gene Autry, Frankie Darro, "Smiley" Burnett and Betsy King Ross, offered a new twist in westerns:

---

[55]William K. Everson, "Movies Out of Thin Air," Films in Review, April, 1955, p. 173.

[56]Ibid. Cf. post, p. 95.

Gene Autry remains his old cowboy self, but right next to his ranch is the entry to "Murania," which is a futuristic civilization existing under the earth. It features such supermodern improvements as robots who do all the work, radium reviving rooms (which came in handy in one episode when Autry turned up dead), and radium generators.[57]

Transatlantic Tunnel (1935) was a British-made picture scripted by Curt Siodmak, starring Richard Dix, Madge Evans, Walter Huston, Basil Sydney and George Arliss. It was "an unrewarding Anglo-American project in which Arliss and Huston made guest appearances as the U. S. President and the British Prime Minister (not Disraeli).[58] The Brandon Films catalogue describes it as ". . . a British film that may be prophetic: the story of a determined engineer and faithful workmen driving through a tunnel between England and the American side."[59]

Science-fiction had invaded the serials with a vengeance by 1936, and Universal produced the first of three fantastic ones based on the exploits of Alex Raymond's popular comic-strip hero, Flash Gordon. In the initial serial, Flash Gordon, Flash and his friends, Dr. Zarkov and Dale Arden (his fiancée), journey in a rocket ship to the planet

---

[57]Don Fabun, "Science Fiction in Motion Pictures, Radio and Television," Modern Science Fiction: Its Meaning and Its Future, Reginald Bretnor, editor (New York: Coward-McCann, 1953), p. 67.

[58]John Springer, "Movie Memory Test: II," Films in Review, May, 1955, pp. 226-227.

[59]1945 Blue List Catalog of Selected Motion Pictures (Brandon Films, Inc. Catalog, 1945. New York: Brandon Films, Inc., 1945),p.12.

Mongo to stop the bombardment of earth by meteorites. There they undergo one hair-raising adventure after another, menaced by monsters, super-scientific inventions and the Emperor Ming, who wants to rule the universe. It was a great success with the Saturday-afternoon popcorn circuit, and still remains "the most inventive and truly fantastic of all surrealist serials. . . ."[60]

> Hollywood's Flash Gordon serials, made in the thirties, satisfy more than all their more ambitious successors, simply because of their abounding innocence and child-like conviction. With joyous relish these inventive fantasies have swallowed every available myth from Méliès onwards. They remain a monument to surrealism. Flash Gordon (Larry "Buster" Crabbe) sets forth as Siegfried . . . again the shining, blonde, Marais-hero in riding-kit astride a rocket ship; landing on Mongo (or Mars) he changes into Superman-kit, complete with lightning-flash insignia and René Creste cape. There he joins battle with Emperor Ming the Merciless (Charles Middleton), a bald Caligari-tyrant wagging a waxed, three pronged beard, and dressed up as Mary Queen of Scots. Remaining true to his perpetual fiancée, Dale Arden, Flash rejects the advances of the blonde, evil Princess Sonia, allying himself instead with the raven-haired Azura, Queen of Magic, who gives him a cloak of invisibility (shades of Siegfried).
>
> The sky, the sea and the underworld are thickly populated with Bird-Men, Rock-Men, Lion-Men and Clay-Men, not to mention an odd unicorn. Ming, a pagan idol-worshipper given to hypnotism, and suffering from an overworked libido where Dale's virginity is concerned, is usually destroyed in Frankenstein-Monster fashion. This leaves him liable to re-emerge at any time and proclaim himself "Emperor of the Universe"—a title, needless to say, that is the safe prerogative of Flash for as long as he stays blonde, shining, and never anything more than affianced.[61]

Directed by Frederick Stephani, this serial was later released in

---

[60] Peter John Dyer, "Some Personal Visions," op. cit., p. 14.

[61] Ibid., p. 31.

feature format under the title Rocket Ship, and has been used often on television.

Only one of the many horror films which Boris Karloff and Bela Lugosi made together in the thirties could really be considered to have overtones of science-fiction. This was The Invisible Ray (1936), produced by Carl Laemmle, Jr. and directed by Lambert Hillyer. In this film, Karloff discovered a strange ray emanating from the constellation Andromeda, which enabled him to look into the past, and eventually led him to the discovery of a new element—Radium X. But this new find brought him nothing but trouble:

> In The Invisible Ray the touch of Karloff's tiniest finger spelled death, for he had become radioactive through contamination by a meteorite rich in radium. He killed his old pal Lugosi before himself catching fire and going up in smoke.[62]

The New York Times took all this with a grain of salt:

> Time marches on. When last we saw Mr. Karloff he was the tragic monster trapped in the tumbling masonry of Frankenstein's mountain laboratory.[63] Karloff has restored the laboratory in The Invisible Ray to its original state and, subleasing it from Frankenstein, has become a scientist on his own. More than that, he has discovered a new element—Radium X—which can blast a boulder at fifty paces, or heal the lame, the halt and the blind at ten.
>
> As the story unreels, you realize that this is just another case

---

[62]Forrest J Ackerman, "The Monster Who Made a Man," Famous Monsters of Filmland, Vol. 1, 1958, p. 32.

[63]This took place in The Bride of Frankenstein (1935), the second in the Frankenstein series.

of a man's manager bringing him along too fast. It is no wonder that Frankenstein's mind cracked under the strain. Becoming poisoned with the new element and acquiring the deadly property of killing everything he touches, he decides to rid the earth of his wife, her lover, the woman he suspects fostered the romance, and the two scientists who revealed Radium X to the world.

Universal, which seems to have a monopoly on films of this sort, has made its newest penny-dreadful with the technical ingenuity and pious hope of frightening the children out of a year's growth. There is evidence, too, that Carl Laemmle wanted to say _boo_ to maturer audiences. In a printed foreword is the legend: "That which you are now to see is a theory whispered in the cloisters of science. Tomorrow these theories may startle the world as fact!" _Boo_ right back at you, Mr. Laemmle![64]

Undersea Kingdom was a 1936 Republic serial, starring Ray "Crash" Corrigan, dealing with a series of fantastic adventures in the lost kingdom of Atlantis. Here, on the bottom of the ocean, Corrigan encountered a weird, super-scientific civilization, complete with disintegrating rays and robots.

But it was up to Britain to produce the most ambitious science-fiction film of the 'thirties, a vast, sprawling film which covered the future of man from the beginning of World War II to the remote year 2036 A. D.[65] _Things to Come_ was adapted from H. G. Wells' book, _The Shape of Things to Come_, by Mr. Wells himself, who also worked closely with Sir Alexander Korda, the producer, and William Cameron

---

[64] _The New York Times_, January 11, 1936.

[65] It is interesting to note that Wells prophesied the date of the beginning of World War II to within one year. Fortunately, he was less accurate concerning its duration.

Menzies, the director, during every phase of the production. This film aroused more speculation and controversy than any science-fiction film since Metropolis. John Grierson offered a penetrating analysis:

> I hope I am not prejudiced by a professional reading of scripts, but I find the published version of Things to Come fascinating and vivid and easy to read.[66] For any one with eyes to see, a film description has many advantages over plain narrative. Events, characterisations and the arguments of the drama are whipped into a running shape more precisely and with less meandering than the narrative form permits. Something certainly is lost. . . . The deviations of description and commentary and plot within plot are impossible. But a mounting action and a tempo'd climax of argument and event give the film description its own virtue. For this alone Things to Come must be a revelation to most people. Here they will see the stuff of which films are made, and, by its origin, it is big stuff which has not often come the way of a film director.
>
> One thing about Wells is that he lives and learns to the minute. I have seen Shaw sink dully, and, for once, dumbly, before a description of the possibilities of cinema. Against this is the vision of Wells sitting watching month after month the wildest experiments the London Film Society could conjure up for him. In so far as he has confessed in my own theatre at the G. P. O. that he was in course of "learning" from us, I may, I hope, claim the right to examine him on this first result.
>
> Let me set down the story in brief and be done with it. In his introductory word, Wells calls it a "spectacle." It is not, like the book The Shape of Things to Come, "a discussion of social and political forces," but a "display" of them; for "a film is no place for argument." The subsequent arguments of its readers and spectators were not the less violent for that. The spectacle is certainly a strange one.

---

[66] H. G. Wells, Things to Come: A Film by H. G. Wells (New York: Macmillan, 1935), 155 pp. Wells published this book version of the screenplay for Things to Come before the film was released. It was entirely different from his original work, The Shape of Things to Come. The film merely used this work as a frame to build on. It is interesting to note how the finished film differs in many ways from the published

It is 1940 or perhaps a little before, and the good families of Everytown are preparing for Christmas. War breaks out and disrupts the families, dragging out from 1940 to 1970. Civilisation disappears and Everytown reverts to mediaeval conditions. The technique of our era of science is lost. The Black Death comes. In the stage of final desolation the reversion to the primitive is complete. Mechanical knowledge is vaguely remembered, and buying and selling is a matter of old clo' bazaars where the effects of the ancient gentry are the prize of bandits' mistresses. The great patriots' war goes on under the leadership of petty chiefs and savage gangsters.

At this point the old Wellsian finger wags, and out of Basra comes a new dominating force which restores civilisation and the world. It is, of course, as every Wellsian knows, the power of the technicians and scientists, mobilised and regimented to reorganise what the politicians and the soldiers, with their imbecile nationalism, have destroyed. As a saving qualification, however, even with the dictatorship of the technicians, perfection does not altogether come. The question of the haves and the have-nots they solve. The deeper question of the do's and the do-nots remains. There is revolution in the Utopia of 2055 [sic]: on the question of whether two young people should be sacrificed by science in a journey to the moon. That revolution is not resolved, and the film ends, as Wells promised, "in a note of interrogation among the stars."

The story goes with a clip, making light of marching armies, landscapes of tanks and poison gas, and scenes of death and desolation as vast as London Town. The chronicle rips over the years of Everytown with the destructive gusto of a tornado making for Miami. "The Tower Bridge of London in ruins. No sign of human life. Seagulls and crows. The Thames, partly blocked with debris, has overflowed its damaged banks." This, one effect in thousands, gives every assurance of spectacle.[67] But one problem drums in

---

screenplay. These differences are chiefly in the form of omissions from the film of dialogue and scenes that were included in the screenplay.

[67]This statement—among others—based on the preceding quotation from the published screenplay of Things to Come, led this writer to the conclusion that Mr. Grierson had in all probability not

my head. Can patriotism be mobilised to its own evident destruction over thirty years? On a more practical and political level, would an armed proletariat stand for it? Wells was not in the war of 1914-18, or he would have sensed how near the breaking-point men can be not in thirty years but in three. The facts are there to guide political philosophy. The Russians broke in three, the Germans in four, and there were, shall we say, certain difficulties appearing among British, French and Italians alike.

It is an important issue for the film, for I doubt if any thesis can sell so vast a dereliction of the human spirit as these thirty years of death and desolation represent. Few at heart will believe in it, and where there is no belief there is only melodrama. On a first impression of the treatment I would say that too much of one's common experience is left out of account. . . .

On a lower level there are other doubts, particularly about these technicians who take the place of the proletariat of Marxist theory and create the first liquidating dictatorship. This is to put faith in a class of society which in the past has shown no inclination to serve any but the highest bidder, and as a class has demonstrated no political consciousness at all. The experts walked out of Russia with their masters. It is an axiom of Marxism that only the proletariat know the burden of Fascism and war, and may be trusted to destroy the system responsible. This one may at least comprehend. That a privileged and honoured class like the experts should find fire and determination enough to give new laws to society is a trifle more difficult to appreciate.

These are the essential issues of Things to Come, and more important than any mere question of film treatment. Being important issues they, of course, affect the treatment considerably. As a result of this lack of faith in the common people there are, for example, no common people in the film, save as soldiers and victims, and no braveries or humanities of common people. A photographic art is, in the last resort, an art of the ordinary. It may by its many fantastic devices create vision and spectacle, but a shot of a child or a spontaneous gesture will bring you slap bang

---

actually seen the finished film when he wrote this critique. The particular scene which he quoted was not included in the film. Neither did he comment on the direction, acting or set design of the film. Perhaps if he had seen the film, he might have had some different reactions to describe.

to cinema's own essential virtue. These scenes of war and pestilence, of a craven or nonexistent people, these star-finding technicians, have not the life's blood of such common observation. They are rather the projection of an argument which one feels is itself out of touch with common observation.

The film reflects this difference. There are marchings and counter-marchings of time—abstract, spectacular, melodramatic, fantastic—but they are no more humanly true than the effects of Metropolis. It is a great story and a great tract, but, if I may say the worst, it is no more intimate in its human reference than a spectacle by de Mille.

There is, of course, the argument that it is high time the spectacles of de Mille found the quality of a great writer and time that we had a great tract in cinema. That miracle has certainly come to pass. There will be more thinking over Things to Come than over any film since Deserter. There is a greater sense of social warning and a better instruction in citizenship than in any previous film whatsoever. It is perhaps the measure of Things to Come that it sets out in most popular fashion to make the millions think. The important thing is that the first of our great writers has taken this medium of millions and studied it and used it to address the world.

. . . .

What I greatly admire is that this brave old master has outfaced us all with the size and scope of his vision, and that this clever old master has seen a way, within the vicious limitations of commercial cinema, to advance a great social argument. Before these two major facts I do not care how unsubtle his sound band is. The mental band is all right, and when, pray, did cinema ever give consideration to that?[68]

Film critic Alistair Cooke found a good deal of fault with the film, but even he reviewed it with grudging admiration in Sight and Sound, but in a manner that did him little credit as a reviewer:

---

[68] John Grierson, "The Cinema of Ideas," Grierson on Documentary, Forsyth Hardy, editor (London and Glasgow: Collins, 1946), pp. 59-63.

The British films this quarter are a proud and, on the whole, a creditable lot. After a good-looking, but dull, first appearance with The Amateur Gentleman and Koenigsberg, . . . our cinema sounded an air-raid warning and Things to Come droned and thundered into our ken. There has been a lot of wrangling about this film. I have done my share and maintain that the acting would be creditable in Madame Tussaud's, the dialogue is pre-war (that little 1914 affair) and that the social psychology is crude materialism. But Vincent Korda and Georges Périnal between them have created at least a half-hour of a world that remains, as a patriotic poet said about an earlier world, "a shining thing in the mind." I don't know what that means, but that makes it all the more apt for Things to Come, which doesn't mean much that is profound but sounds tremendous and looks a million dollars—or more. Its faults are defections from the standards we film critics carry round with us waiting to fire off at the first adult film that comes our way. There have been not more than a dozen or so in twenty years, and it may be some compliment to Things to Come to say that it at least gets our hand on the trigger.[69]

Mr. Wells' Things to Come is, above all, spectacular. But it is unlike the run of "spectacle" films, such as Cecil B. de Mille's, with their teeming casts and ultra-gorgeous settings, that excite the eye and stun the imagination and culminate in some monster cataclysm. The technique of Things to Come is controlled and quiet, the cast, all things considered, unexpectedly small; the actors being used with such intelligence that not a figure appears without effect.[70] Though the horrors of war, most notably an air raid on an Everytown that is the London of to-day, appear in the film early, Things to Come is memorable not for its use of horror, its power to wring the nerves, but for its command of two important elements: size and rhythm. Detail is used also, with feeling and precision, but dramatic use of detail is not an innovation; it is for its power to present size emotionally, to make one feel either an object or an event to be unprecedented, extraordinary, that this

---

[69] Alistair Cooke, "Films of the Quarter," Sight and Sound, Spring, 1936, pp. 24-25.

[70] The cast included such distinguished actors as Raymond Massey (who played two roles), Sir Ralph Richardson as the warlike "Boss," and Sir Cedric Hardwicke as Theotocopulos, the artisan-rebel of the future metropolis.

film seems to me chiefly remarkable. . . . Machines and buildings seldom command the screen, dwarf the actor or make us feel their majesty; here they do.

Mr. Wells is a romanticist with a vital attitude towards science. He is an artist with a profound mistrust of art. He is a humanitarian and a moralist first of all: his conception of Things to Come lacks both the sternness and the frivolity of an artist's. If the film has a "message," it shows that passion wrecks us, that it is fatal to rate too high a person or an illusion.

. . . .

The opening passages of the film are realistic (and, consequently, unnerving); the middle is picaresque, with rescues and counterplots. The end seemed pure fantasy; its intention was (at least by me) forgotten in an amused delight of the eye. As the story marches on into the future, ever further from a present that we know as reality, it becomes more abstract. The material, at its outset, is the familiar; at its close, the unknown: then images have to be at once amazing and possible. In making sets for the future Mr. Vincent Korda had so much scope that he might well have lost his head. He seems to me to have kept it admirably. Size—as I said before—and a kind of inexorability make the mise-en-scene of 2036 impressive. . . .[71]

If this film fully came off it might knock one flat; it does not fully come off because of a constant conflict between moral and poetic intention. It tries to be too comprehensive; its aims are confused. Mr. Alexander Korda has worked magnificently, but he, too, was perplexed, or allowed himself to be side-tracked. All the same, Things to Come is a film that grows in the memory. It should be seen for its rolling boldness, the excellence of its lighting, its naivety, its drama and the unforgettable beauty of some of the shots.[72]

Even the musical score for Things to Come was revolutionary, as John

---

[71] Mr. Korda's assistant art director on this film was none other than Mr. Wells' son, Frank Wells.

[72] Elizabeth Bowen, "Things to Come: A Critical Appreciation," Sight and Sound, Spring, 1936, pp. 10-12.

Huntley mentions in his book, British Film Music:

> Appropriately enough, it was Muir Mathieson himself who initiated the great film music event in 1935 which brought the first five years of film music development in Great Britain to a climax and had a widespread effect on all subsequent progress, the event that first brought film music to the attention of the serious music lovers of this and other countries, the score that even today holds a unique position in any history of film music—Things to Come. This picture was one of the most ambitious projects ever attempted by British film units and remains today as one of the major achievements of Alexander Korda's London Films company.[73]

Mr. Wells tried a second venture into cinema the following year, and The Man Who Could Work Miracles was a delightfully fantastic adaptation of his short story about George McWhirter Fotheringay (Roland Young), who is suddenly given the power to perform miracles by "three super-beings in outer space—one of them played by George Sanders—who discuss the potentialities and limitations of mankind."[74] The film was more fantasy than science-fiction and Alexander Korda again produced. Sir Ralph Richardson was again starred, along with Roland Young, Ernest Thesiger, George Zucco and George Sanders.

Russia produced The Last Night in 1937, and Universal came up with a rather boring film in which Boris Karloff played—surprisingly enough—a sympathetic role! In Night Key he was a scientist whose invention was stolen by criminals.

---

[73] John Huntley, British Film Music (London: Skelton Robinson, 1947), pp. 39-40.

[74] Edward Conner, "Angels on the Screen," Films in Review, August-September, 1958, p. 379.

In 1938 Ford Beebe and Robert Hill directed the second of the popular Flash Gordon serials, Flash Gordon's Trip to Mars. Once again Buster Crabbe as Flash Gordon rocketed into the unknown to save the world from the mad Emperor Ming. This one proved so popular that it was cut into feature format that same year and released under the title, Mars Attacks the World. Look magazine also ran a picture-story of the serial for several weeks, consolidating several chapters into one each week. A description of the opening chapter from this magazine series will demonstrate how similar the plot of this second serial was to the first:[75]

> Riding a strange ray with the speed of light (186,000 miles a second), two giant men from Mars hurtle from the heavens toward earth in the opening scenes of this 15-part serial. . . . Landing on earth, far from civilization, under cover of night, the Martians plant a strange device in the earth's surface, then die, 35 million miles from home, killed by the earth's dense atmosphere. On Mars, evil Emperor Ming of the mythical planet Mongo, who has joined with Mars' Queen Azura to capture the universe, watches the earth from a giant observatory. In a rocket ship, Flash Gordon heads for Mars, to save the earth from doom, as the device the Martians planted has set up a ray sucking earth's nitrogen away. As the rocket speeds away, Flash (Buster Crabbe) discovers a stowaway, a newspaper photographer (Donald Kerr). Flash's friends, the scientist, Dr. Zarkov (Frank Shannon) and Dale Arden (Jean Rogers), look on in amazement. Nearing the red globe of Mars, the rocket travelers look out upon a strange, turreted city. Here, Dr. Zarkov believes, must be the giant ray lamp which has been making contact with the device the two martyr Martians planted in the earth, causing earthquakes and cyclones, foretelling doom. To wreck this giant lamp is the purpose of the 5,000 miles-an-hour trip to Mars in the awe-inspiring rocket. But

---

[75] Cf. ante, p. 51.

Mars is wary of strangers. A nitrogen gun fires at Flash's rocket ship from a fantastic powerhouse. In the Valley of Desolation the stricken rocket lands, to be attacked by Queen Azura's bombing strato-sleds. Fleeing from the bombers, Flash and his friends dash into a nearby cave, only to be trapped as a strange wall suddenly lowers from the ceiling. From behind the wall appear weird men of clay, who offer freedom only if Flash can force Queen Azura to restore the clay men to their former flesh and blood selves. When the clay men release Flash and Zarkov (whose clothes have been changed into Martian costumes by magic), the two overpower one of the queen's bombing sled pilots and fly to the palace. Here, on her throne, Queen Azura (Beatrice Roberts) realizes she is trapped. When she clutches at a magic sapphire, Flash seizes her. As Flash carries the queen across one of the strange bridges of light from the palace to the strato-sled landing tower, Emperor Ming (Charles Middleton) discovers the plot, turns a disintegrating ray on the tower. As it collapses, Flash leaps to safety with Azura, but then is recaptured by her soldiers. When Flash and Zarkov refuse to aid Ming and Azura in conquering the universe, Ming orders them thrown into the fiery lamp of Mars—the same one which is destroying the earth. As the captives are led to the great cauldron, however, they break away. Flash escapes in a strato-sled after taking time to wreck the lamp. Back inthe cave, the Clay Men think he has betrayed them.[76]

Another serial produced the same year, The Lost City, concerned the nefarious activities of a mad doctor in a lost jungle city who used super-scientific devices to change the natives into brainless monsters. Its sole claim to notoriety was the fact that it was banned in Lithuania "because of 'inhuman treatment.' "[77]

The Gladiator (Columbia, 1938) was a feature bearing the same

---

[76]"Flash Gordon's Trip to Mars," Look, March 15, 1938, pp. 59-61.

[77]John Eugene Harley, World-Wide Influences of the Cinema (Los Angeles: University of Southern California Press, 1940), p. 162.

title as Philip Wylie's novel about a man endowed with superhuman powers, but there the resemblance ceased:

> . . . when the word went around that a film was to be made of Philip Wylie's Gladiator, science fiction fans familiar with its very virile superman hero and his sexy performances everywhere from canoes to bedroom cots, wondered how the picture'd get past the Hays Office—the cinema censorship bureau of the time. The answer was simple: instead of a serious scientifilm they made a slapstick scientifarce, a not-so-wily treatment of the Wylie novel that bore little resemblance to the original.[78]

As the decade closed, another serial appeared, also starring Buster Crabbe, but was only a poor copy of the original Flash Gordon's: Buck Rogers (Universal, 1939). And as the flames of World War II—just as H. G. Wells had foretold, three years before—began to spread across the face of Europe, Richard Pottier directed a film in France called Le Monde tremblera (The World Will Tremble), "whose title, at least, was prophetic."[79]

By 1940 the science-fiction film, as such, was fast becoming lost in the shuffle of horror films from Hollywood. The two terms were almost interchangeable in audiences' minds, and with good reason. Only a few borderline cases are of interest to us here. Flash Gordon Conquers the Universe (Universal, 1940) was the last of the "pure" science-fictions for some time, and also the last of the Flash Gordon serials. The plot and characters had at last worn thin.

---

[78] Ackerman, "Confessions of a Science Fiction Addict," loc.cit.

[79] Michel Laclos, op. cit., p. xxxi.

Besides The Invisible Killer (PRC, 1940) this first year of the new decade did produce one rather ambitious film—and in Technicolor. Paramount's Dr. Cyclops was written by Curt Siodmak and Henry Kuttner, old-time pro in the field of science-fiction, and directed by Ernest B. Schoedsack of King Kong fame. Albert Dekker, as "a shave-pate, myopic, 6'-2" maverick scientist"[80] experimented with the idea of reducing human beings in size. The film "recounts with a slight flavor of sadism, what goes on"[81] when Dr. Cyclops

> . . . founds a laboratory in the darkest technicolored interior of the Amazon and becomes obsessed with the mania to reduce his colleagues to a height of thirteen inches thru overexposure to specialized radium treatment.
>
> Janice Logan, Thomas Coley, Charles Halton, and Victor Killian, as the Tom Thumb guinea pigs, conceal their nakedness with the help of some loose-fitting handkerchiefs and tirelessly plot a way out of their embarrassing predicament. They find a solution by accidentally smashing the sleeping doctor's thick-lensed spectacles, and send him raging wildly about the laboratory in his myopic helplessness, stalking his elusive tormentors and ultimately winding up at the bottom of the radium pit. The doctor's colleagues, gloating over his demise, regain their normal stature after due exposure to sunlight and air, then naturally prepare to return to a less hazardous environment in the States.[82]
>
> . . . But realism and fantasy seldom mix, even in the Amazon jungle. Result: the plight of the miniature actors dodging for

---

[80]"Cinema," Time, April 8, 1940, p. 83.

[81]Ibid.

[82]Jack Nealon, "An Historical and Critical Survey of the American Horror Film Since 1930" (unpublished Master's thesis, The University of Southern California, Los Angeles, 1953), pp. 99-100.

> their lives behind a huge can of pork and beans, peering up at a towering rooster or laboriously sawing themselves slices of garguantuan baloney, is less frightening than funny.[83]

The Man-Made Monster (Universal, 1941) brought us a high-voltage Frankenstein Monster with a death-dealing touch and hands and face that glowed eerily in the dark.

> Circus star Lon Chaney, Jr., has developed a phenomenal resistance to electric shock, but none at all to Dr. Lionel Atwill, who wants to ensnare him in a maniacal scheme. Atwill feeds him several thousand volts of electricity, induces him to commit murder, and even lets him cheat death in the electric chair. When Chaney wins a match with the hot-seat, he starts to glow with the brilliance of a carbon arc, scorches human prey with the ease of a turbulent fuse-box, then dissipates his power-house energy when he gets entangled in the twisting intricacies of a barbed-wire fence.[84]

Raketenflug zum Mond (Rocket Flight to the Moon) (1941) was the first foreign science-fiction film since 1939. A rather obscure film, this one was made in Bavaria.

The Lady and the Monster (Republic, 1944) was the unfortunate title attached to quite an interesting film, based on the Curt Siodmak novel, Donovan's Brain.

> Donovan's Brain, the Curt Siodmak horror novel which was published to critical plaudits early last year (1943), lost an intriguing title and a large portion of plausibility and pace in the chiller based on it. . . . The Lady and the Monster stems from the premise that a brain once separated from its parent body and kept alive, may transmit its thought processes to humans via telepathy. As that eminent researcher, Professor Erich von Stroheim

---

[83]"Cinema," Time, loc. cit.

[84]Nealon, op. cit., p. 102.

> explains: "When you are trying to solve the mysteries of nature, it doesn't matter whether you experiment with humans or guinea pigs." The writers and cast take it from there. In a castle set in an Arizona desert, von Stroheim and his assistants, Vera Hruba Ralston and Richard Arlen, proceed to test the theory by stealing the brain of . . . W. H. Donovan . . . who has just been killed in an airplane crash. Most of the accredited appurtenances of the medical thriller are from the test-tube-filled laboratory to the operating table. As additional fill-ins there are a wrong-accused murderer, a missing fortune, and Mr. Arlen walking about in a zombie-like trance, under the influence of Donovan's brain. It should be noted that Mr. Arlen's performance is the most credible of the lot. But the truth is, *The Lady and the Monster* is a mite too lethargic. In this case, Donovan's brain could stand a shot of adrenalin.[85]

However, the film was a cut or two above the usual thriller, probably because there was a good, suspenseful novel to base it on. Alton Cook in *The New York World Telegram* called it "definitely one of the . . . most engrossing and mature mystery pictures."[86] Otis Guernsay stated that "hidden under this conventional nomenclature is one of the most hair-raising of films,"[87] and Jack Nealon observed that

> *The Lady and the Monster* proved to be a sleeper. Little publicized, the film caused small bickering among the critics. . . . *The Lady and the Monster* had its superior moments, notably the careful way in which it handled the growing menace of the brain before the powerless trio who nurtured it into being . . .[88]

Donovan's Brain has proved to be a popular story down through the

---

[85] *The New York Times*, April 8, 1944.

[86] *The New York World Telegram*, April 7, 1944.

[87] *The New York Herald Tribune*, April 7, 1944.

[88] Nealon, *op. cit.*, pp. 103-104.

years. It was remade in 1953 with Lew Ayres, and has been done on television at least once.

They Came to a City (1944) proved to be the first serious science-fiction picture since Things to Come, as once again British film-makers decided to use the medium of cinema to make people think a bit. Unfortunately, this strange film experiment was not too successful, either as food for thought or as an entertainment. Based on a novel by J. B. Priestley, the film was directed by Basil Dearden. The New Yorker said of it:

> They Came to a City features Mr. J. B. Priestley in person, complete with pipe, apparently in one of his more evangelical moods. It seems that he wants to talk about Walt Whitman's "dream of a new city of friends," where ideal social conditions prevail. In the story he tells, to quote my handmaiden, "Nine people with various environments step out of them into a dark night, accompanied by the clash of cymbals. They wander down a foggy road, hung over with naked branches, until they come to a courtyard full of angular objects and a curious door bearing an enormous star in bas-relief. Music plays, the door swings open, and one by one they go in. You never actually see the city, but the idea generally is that some like it and some don't, depending mostly on their political theories. In the end, two simple people, a sailor and his girl, go back to report to the world on Mr. Priestley's Utopia. Favorably. The cast includes Googie Withers, John Clements, and A. E. Matthews.[89]

Croisières sidérales (Sidereal Cruises) (1945), was a French effort by André Zwobada and Pierre Guerlais which Michel Laclos

---

[89] "The Current Cinema," The New Yorker, February 24, 1945, p. 55.

called "a lamentably poor thing."[90]

White Pongo (PRC, 1945) was a jungle "thriller" which concerned itself with an expedition searching for the "missing link" between ape and man, a huge white gorilla with "almost human" intelligence. This film was so badly and cheaply made as to be almost unbelievable:

> A cheap PRC thriller of a few years back, White Pongo, included a sequence of two (phoney) gorillas battling, intercut with stock shots of jungle denizens watching the struggle with the greatest of interest. Among the usual scenes of chattering monkeys and screeching birds was a delightful shot of King Kong sitting in the foliage quite unconcerned by it all. His benign expression was probably the reason Schoedsack and Cooper had junked the scene back in 1933![91]

The remainder of 1945 and 1946 saw the production of only a few pseudoscientific horror films and serials, such as The Purple Monster Strikes (1945); The Monster and the Ape (1945), which featured a huge robot with glowing eyes; The Crimson Ghost (1946), in which a skull-masked fiend neutralized all electricity with a machine called a "cyclotrode"; The Invisible Informer (1946); and The Flying Serpent (1946), in which George Zucco's pet, a giant flying snake, kept everybody away from some treasure in the desert.

Finally, somebody realized that that thing which exploded on

---

[90] Laclos, op. cit., p. xxxii.

[91] William K. Everson, "Movies Out of Thin Air," Films in Review, April, 1955, pp. 177-178.

Hiroshima and Nagisaki in 1945 might be good material for a movie. So MGM whipped up a showy production that turned out to be more science-fiction than the producers perhaps intended. The Beginning or the End, as Life put it, "exploded with a pseudoscientific pop."[92]

> At last, Hollywood has got hold of atomic energy. With great fanfare, Metro-Goldwyn-Mayer, the biggest company in the business, is releasing a picture called The Beginning or The End as fulfillment of its self-assumed "rare responsibility" to portray on the screen the development of the atomic bomb. To give the film authenticity, payments were made to prominent nuclear physicists for permission to impersonate them in it. Ultimately the producers got so carried away with their brainchild that a "newsreel" preamble was tacked on, recommending The Beginning or the End as documented fact to the 25th Century and, by implication, to the present generation as well.
>
> Unfortunately, those who expect to learn much about the atom in Hollywood's school will be disappointed or misled. M-G-M has sandwiched the development of atomic energy between slabs of a stale love story in which a young scientist indicates to his unhappy wife that he'd be home for dinner more often if it weren't so darned hard to figure out this chain-reaction stuff. Nuclear physics is often misrepresented by simplifying it to the level of an Erector set, and some of the historic scenes, like those involving the late President Roosevelt, are considerably over dramatized. Serious consideration of the implications of the unleashed atom is confined to brief dialog ("I can't help wondering if we're right.") accompanied by a far-away look in the eyes.
>
> Although The Beginning or the End has an agreeable air of excitement and includes impressive moments that cannot be laughed off—like those at Alamogordo and Hiroshima—it has destroyed itself by an overdose of what Hollywood considers "popular appeal." A bad drama to begin with, inaccurate documentation deprives this movie of the authoritative quality which

---

[92] "The Beginning or the End," Life, March 17, 1947, p. 75.

M-G-M claims for it.[93]

The comics moved into the movie world in 1947 in full force. Brick Bradford (Columbia, 1947) joined the roster of Flash Gordon and Buck Rogers, and Dick Tracy's latest screen venture, Dick Tracy Meets Gruesome (RKO, 1947), involved a little mad scientist who invented bombs that could stop all movement instantaneously within a certain radius. This allowed the gangster "Gruesome" (Boris Karloff) to walk right into a bank and out again with a basket full of money, under the noses of frozen bank guards. Aside from this "science-fiction" gimmick, the rest of the film was routine cops-and-robbers.

The third comic-strip hero to make his movie debut was the ever-popular Superman. Created in 1939 as a syndicated strip, by 1947 he had become so popular that

> Paramount Pictures, Inc., signed a contract to distribute a series of technicolor animated cartoon shorts to be produced by the Max Fleischer Studios. These will be released at the rate of one a month for three years.[94]

They were rather successful at the time, and marked the first use of animation for "serious" science-fiction, i.e., as opposed to the "funny-animals" school of cartoons.

---

[93] Ibid.

[94] Martin Sheridan, Comics and Their Creators (Boston: Ralph T. Hale and Company, 1942), p. 234. Superman's claim to the science-fiction category stems from the fact that he originally came here from another planet. This accounts for his incredible feats of

The following year, Superman became a flesh-and-blood hero in a live-action serial directed by Spencer Bennett and Thomas Carr. Aside from the opening chapter, which portrayed Superman's origin and escape to earth from his exploding home world of Krypton, the serial was a great disappointment to the many Superman fans. Kirk Alyn was too flabby and his uniform too baggy; the acting and direction were atrocious and the plot was worse. And the crowning blow came when Superman got ready to fly: apparently unable to extricate himself completely from the world of pen-and-ink, he turned into an _animated figure_ and zoomed away into the sky!

Unknown Island (Film Classics, 1948) was an up-to-date version of _The Lost World_, but the silent version proved vastly superior to this Cinecolored nightmare of papier-maché dinosaurs and fuzzy orange gorillas. Barton McLane, Virginia Grey, Richard Denning and Philip Reed had a fine time lobbing grenades at tyrannosauri, battling a "giant sloth" (the orange gorilla), and killing each other off on a forgotten prehistoric island in the South Seas.

---

strength and his "X-ray vision." Years ago, it seems, the planet Krypton—a world in another solar system—exploded from interior disturbances, and only one of its inhabitants was saved. Superman, then a Superbaby, was shot off into space just before the cataclysm in a rocket ship launched by his parents, who hoped to give him at least some chance for survival. He landed on earth, was adopted by a kindly family named Kent, and grew into Supermanhood with them. Somehow he managed to keep his super powers secret all those years, and at maturity he began to use them to fight crime and criminals on his adopted planet.

King of the Rocket Men (Columbia, 1949) was another of "Jungle Sam" Katzman's serials,[95] starring Tristram Coffin, Mae Clarke and Don Haggerty. This one had Katzman's sure-fire money-making formula and puerile special effects, just like all the rest: "Scientist combats a madman who seeks to rule the earth."[96] This one was later put into feature format and released in 1951 under the title Lost Planet Airmen.

Project X (Film Classics, 1949) was a Swedish-made borderline science-fiction film, starring Keith Andes and Jack Lord, but lest the decade end without a little something on the spectacular side, RKO repeated the old success formula of King Kong and released Mighty Joe Young. Produced by John Ford and Merian C. Cooper, the old King Kong gang joined forces once again to unleash some giant monkey business. Ernest B. Schoedsack again directed, and the capable special effects were again handled by veteran Willis O'Brien. As an added attraction, the film's climactic sequences were tinted!

> Mighty Joe Young, a fine piece of action-fantasy, provides the most stupendous spectacle of simian shenanigans since King Kong defied attacking airplanes from the mooring mast of the Empire State Building (1933). Its trick photography is admirable, its

---

[95] Mr. Katzman, better known as Jungle Sam, has earned a reputation as Hollywood's only independent producer whose films—though all despised by the critics—have never lost money. "Meet Jungle Sam," Life, March 23, 1953, p. 79.

[96] Steven H. Scheuer, TV Movie Almanac and Ratings, 1958 and 1959 (New York: Bantam Books, 1958), p. 120.

> whopping implausibility almost impeccable. Best of all, it is such a gigantic, reckless spoof, that it is practically irresistible.
>
> Unlike the ferocious Kong, Gorilla Joe Young is as lovable as a Saint Bernard. He worships his jungle mistress (Terry Moore) and obeys her every word. It is only when he becomes the target of a safari, headed by Robert Armstrong,[97] that he begins to throw his weight around. Captured by Armstrong's cowboys, who look like Lilliputian dare-devils mounted on pygmy horses, Joe is bundled off to Hollywood as a nightclub attraction.
>
> His stay in the U. S. is a stormy one, highlighted by: 1) a tug of war with a string of overaged strongmen (including Primo Carnera, Phil ["Swedish Angel"] Olafsson, and Man Mountain Dean); 2) an ear-splitting rampage in which Joe reduces the nightclub to kindling; and 3) the lurid rescue of a tot in a nightie from a burning orphanage.[98]

Unlike his predecessor, Joe is a hero at the end of the picture, and goes back to Africa to live to a beamingly happy ripe old age.

Thus ended two decades which had seen a depression, a world war and a fantastic new weapon of destruction, the atomic bomb. The public was gradually becoming aware that science was making great strides, and treading hard on the heels of science-fiction. There had been a great many good films produced, but even more that, unfortunately, were not so good. So it was indeed welcome when the increased scientific awareness sparked a new renaissance of adult science-fiction films in the 'fifties.

---

[97] Armstrong apparently had not learned his lesson from King Kong in 1933.

[98] "Cinema," Time, August 8, 1949, p. 70.

III. THE RENAISSANCE OF THE SCIENCE-FICTION FILM: 1950 TO 1955

Nineteen fifty was a year of great importance in the history of the science-fiction film. For it was in that year that Hungarian-born producer George Pal, long famous for his "Puppetoons" and other unusual films, made the first seriously authentic science-fiction film of space flight, Destination Moon. Louis Berg calls it

> . . . the first Hollywood fantasy ever to soar off into space from a platform of real scientific speculation.
>
> Before he [Pal] pepped up the field, Hollywood's ventures in the field of science-fiction were of the old fashioned variety. The thriller-chiller specialists out on the Coast never got much further than the quaint 19th-century notions of Frankenstein, Dracula, vampires and zombies. When this limited Gothic vein threatened to peter out, they resorted to clumsy sequels—Bride of Frankenstein, Son of Dr. Jekyll, etc.
>
> Destination Moon got away from the philters and potions, it abandoned the old-time chemical laboratory for the supersonic, electronic, atomic science of tomorrow. Others followed suit.[99]

Destination Moon, filmed in Technicolor, was indeed a different and impressive film. Directed by the late Irving Pichel, it was based loosely on the novel Rocket Ship Galileo, by Robert A. Heinlein, veteran science-fiction writer, who also collaborated on the screenplay. Astronomer and science-fiction author Dr. R. S. Richardson told how the film came to be made:

---

[99] Louis Berg, "Hollywood Discovers Mars," This Week, Sept. 14, 1952, p. 9.

Not until very recently . . . did the motion pictures discover science fiction. There have been plenty of horror pictures, some fantasy pictures, and a few on the borderline like The Lost World, One Million B. C., and The Invisible Man. But no trips to the moon or invasions from Saturn. If you didn't like gangsters or musicals, you could stay home and read Jules Verne.

Now all this has suddenly changed. Happy days are here again for character actors who can play astronomers and girls who can look glamorous while solving a third-order differential equation. Astronomers themselves are being routed out of their ivory towers. Scarcely a week goes by without some studio calling up for information on the inner workings of an observatory or how long it takes to determine the orbit of a new asteroid or comet.

. . . .

A year or more ago George Pal produced Destination Moon, based upon a novel by Robert Heinlein. . . . Few people probably realize what a risky venture it seemed at that time. It was a picture with no big names in the cast, with a radically new theme from that which audiences had been accustomed. The science-fiction fans could naturally be counted upon to turn out in force. But how about the bobby-soxers and the tired women shoppers? How about the middle-aged family trade euphemistically referred to by theatre managers as the Serutan group? Would a title like Destination Moon mean anything to them? Nobody knew till it hit the screen.

I have been told that the response surpassed the most optimistic predictions. The public was found to be not only ready and waiting for pictures of this kind, but eager to see bold extrapolations into the future. But they had to be well done. The science must be authentic, the characters and situations convincing, and the trick stuff done with careful attention to detail. There is no critic so hostile as the amateur scientist hot on the trail of a technical error.

. . . .

. . . I asked Pal point-blank how he happened to produce Destination Moon in the first place.

"Well, you see I have two boys who happen to be very fond of science fiction. From listening to them I began to get interested in

> it myself. One night at a party I met Robert Heinlein who told me what a great picture could be made about a trip to the Moon. I tried to interest others in the idea but it was a long time before I found anyone with money who was willing to back such a picture."[100]

But he did find backers, and for two years Pal labored on his film to make sure it would be minutely accurate as well as entertaining. Then, in 1950:

> It hit the screens of the land backed by all the fanfare and hoopla accorded a major studio release, and went out over theater circuits which held a large share of the audience. It was an immediate success and on its first run-through, picked up \$1,800,000 in United States and Canadian showings and an additional \$1,000,000 in British theaters. Science fiction had come to Hollywood.
>
> Practically everyone with more than a passing interest in science fiction is familiar with the story of the production; the special sets and gimmicks; the problems of lighting and space suits and all the rest. Technically, the picture was as accurate as Hollywood could make it, aided and abetted by a team of experts, and only the most carping purist could find very much to be unhappy about. In essence, the picture was a documentary. It lacked story—or rather, what story it had was based on the rather unreasonable assumption that the engineering that could build a successful moon rocket in the first place was inadequate to the task of figuring a high enough safety factor and sufficient return fuel. But it drew American audiences, millions of whom knew of science-fiction themes only through comic books and hypoed space operas. It drew them because it was novel, it was a tremendous spectacle, it was given a tremendous build-up in the press, and because it capitalized on a growing public awareness that modern technology and science fiction were running just about neck and neck.

Destination Moon was an artistic success as well as a box-office success. Bosley Crowther, astute movie critic for the _New_

---

[100] R. S. Richardson, "Making Worlds Collide," _Astounding Science Fiction_, November, 1951, pp. 84, 96.

> York Times, listed Destination Moon as one of the "Ten Best Pictures" of 1950, picking also a British release that bordered on science-fiction, but was actually a suspense thriller, Seven Days to Noon.[101] Destination Moon was the first science-fiction picture to win an award by the Academy of Motion Picture Arts and Sciences, presented to George Pal Productions and Eagle-Lion Classics in 1950 for "Special Effects." . . . Box-office and critical recognition and artistic success, all rolled up in one picture, is a combination that opens the doors of Hollywood.[102]

But in spite of its technical accuracy, Destination Moon had many faults, story-wise, such as were pointed out by Holiday:

> Pal showed us what the movies could do with science fiction in his Destination Moon. Admittedly, Destination Moon had a wretched plot, wooden acting and generally poor construction throughout; yet the believability of its rocket-in-space sequences lifted it out of the run of B-pictures and won hearts of both critical science-fiction fans and average movie goers. . . .[103]

Actually, Destination Moon was not the pioneer that science-fiction fans like to think it, as far as actual release goes. But it certainly was in conception and originality. Robert L. Lippert, always alert for a good thing, got wind of Pal's plans for Destination Moon, saw that here was a new type of film that might compete with the inroads television was making on movie audiences, and rushed one of his own to completion. Rocketship X-M was finished in about half the time

---

[101] Infra, p. 80.

[102] Don Fabun, "Science Fiction in Motion Pictures, Radio and Television," Modern Science Fiction: Its Meaning and Its Future, Reginald Bretnor, editor (New York: Coward-McCann, 1953), pp. 51-52.

[103] Al Hine, "Pagans and Planets," Holiday, November, 1951, p. 26.

and for about half the cost of Destination Moon, and looked it. It was released just before Destination Moon, or in many cases, simultaneously. As a result, it was quite successful.[104]

> The word successful is used in its Hollywood sense, and has little to do with the disapprobation with which more experienced science-fiction fans greeted it. Rocket Ship X-M cost only $94,000 to produce, a drop in the king-sized Hollywood bucket, and by October, 1951, when it had run through its circuits, had picked up $700,000 in box-office receipts; a fairly respectable figure and one that made Hollywood take a second look at science fiction.[105]

Despite the lack of technical accuracy in this film, there was a little more story, and the critics were not unimpressed:

> Add to such Hollywood formulas as the musical and the Western, a new type of picture—the Solaropera, which uses the planetary system for its great outdoors and the rocketship for its trusty steed. With a cycle of such astral adventure stories under way, Rocketship X-M comes in first with the pseudo-scientific pattern that sounds glib, mystifying, and infinitely more plausible than it did in the days of Jules Verne.
>
> In Rocketship Lloyd Bridges, Osa Massen, John Emery, Noah Beery Jr., and the rest take off for the moon in the interest of pure science, but a slight impurity in their calculations lands them on Mars instead. This gives Kurt Neumann, the film's writer-director-producer, a chance to point a moral: Mars is a radioactive wasteland inhabited by the brutish survivors of an ancient atomic war. But chiefly Neumann uses his scientific mumbo-jumbo for melodrama, and the rest is a workmanlike development

---

[104] Richard Gehman, "The Hollywood Horrors," Cosmopolitan, November, 1958, p. 41, In this article the film's producer-director-writer himself, the late Kurt Neumann, talks about the making of Rocketship X-M.

[105] Fabun, loc. cit.

of a fascinating theme.[106]

Superman returned to the screen in a new Columbia serial that was even more ridiculous than the first one. _Atom Man Vs. Superman_ (1950) pitted the "Man of Steel" against somebody called Atom Man, who puttered around in a laboratory full of flashing lights and jiggling dials, wearing a black robe and what looked like a tin bucket on his head.

The Flying Saucer (Film Classics, 1950) was a quickie production made to capitalize on the interest in flying saucers about that time, in which

> An undercover investigator for the government journies [sic] to Alaska to find out about those flying saucers, runs into Commie spies there.[107]

The Perfect Woman (Eagle-Lion, 1950) was a British comedy farce about a scientist who constructs a robot woman and then hires a man-about-town to try her out in public. Director Bernard Knowles let the whole thing get pretty silly, rather than funny, and actors Patricia Roc, Stanley Holloway and Nigel Patrick seemed to be having a better time than the audience.[108]

El Sexo Fuerte (_The Strong Sex_)(Casa Films, 1950) was a

---

[106] "Movies," _Newsweek_, June 5, 1950, p. 86.

[107] Scheuer, _op. cit._, p. 65.

[108] _Ibid._, p. 161.

Mexican scientifarce, and Two Lost Worlds (United Artists, 1950) was a soporific hodge-podge of stock footage starring James Arness:

> A colony from Australia lands on a mysterious isle where prehistoric monsters roam. Low grade thriller; if you're a TV movie fan, you'll spot stock footage from Captain Fury, One Million B. C. and Captain Caution used to stretch the budget.[109]

In Britain Roy and John Boulting produced an extraordinary suspense thriller about "a deranged atomic scientist who threatens to blow up London if they fail to do his bidding."[110] There may be some doubt as to whether Seven Days to Noon (1950) was really science-fiction, but there was no doubt that it was good cinema:

> A top British atomic scientist, in acute moral distress over his work, sends an ultimatum to No. 10 Downing Street: unless the government publicly renounces the manufacture of atom bombs within seven days, he will set one off in the heart of midday London. The discovery that Professor Willingdon (Barry Jones) is indeed missing from his government laboratory—along with a potent U. R. 12 that could fit into his small satchel—touches off a major crisis in London and a major moviemaking feat . . .
>
> The Boultings have succeeded in persuading London itself to act out the crisis as if it were really happening. Their film uses striking documentary detail, a wealth of British character bits; it uses no twists or gimmicks to spoil a logical, harrowing account of how the metropolis tries to head off its doom and at the same time prepare to meet it.
>
> . . . .
>
> Though it gives human, often humorous, color to the grim story, the film never compromises its chilling realism with the conventions of movie fiction. . . . the real heroine of Seven Days is

---

[109] Ibid., p. 224.

[110] Ibid., p. 184.

> London, with its streets, landmarks, and citizens. The city gives a terrifyingly good performance.[111]

Abbott and Costello Meet the Invisible Man (Universal, 1951) killed off the poor old Invisible Man once and for all, just as Abbott and Costello had done for Frankenstein's Monster, Dracula and the Wolf Man three years earlier in Abbott and Costello Meet Frankenstein (1948). Jack Nealon called the former picture "a slapdash spoofing of psychiatric madness and fumbling gangsterism."[112]

By now, spurred on by the obvious financial rewards to be gained from this "new" financial bonanza, science-fiction, small producers as well as major studios were rushing productions to completion. RKO's Captive Women (1951) is a case in point. It was originally titled 3000 A. D., but this title being a little tame for the distributors, it was changed to the more lurid one mentioned above.

> The latest in the current vogue for world disaster movies, 3000 A. D., was readied for release by RKO. It presents a nightmarish picture of life 10 centuries hence, when the U. S. has been destroyed by atomic wars and people live Stone Age lives.
>
> A tribe living in the wreckage of New York City wars with a tribe across the Hudson River—the "mutates" who inherited radiation-caused disfigurements. The mutates discover the abandoned Holland Tunnel, use it to abduct Manhattan's normal women.
>
> Finally, a non-disfigured mutate boy meets a "norm" girl, loses girl, gets girl—and they start a happier race

---

[111] "Cinema," Time, December 25, 1950, p. 56.

[112] Nealon, op. cit., p. 90.

together.[113]

Starring Robert Clarke, Gloria Saunders and Ron Randell, this film was re-released in 1957 under yet another title: 1000 Years from Now.

The Man from Planet X (1951) was United Artists' bid, shot in a few days for almost nothing, and raking in quite a handsome profit for its producers, Aubrey Wisberg and Jack Pollexfen. Because it was one of the first in this "new trend," it even got a nice picture spread in Life,[114] and was released in a comic magazine version.

> United Artists released The Man from Planet X, of which the New York Times said, The Man from Planet X landed at the Mayfair on Saturday and he and the picture make up one of the most excruciating bores ever to emerge from that pinpoint on this planet known as Hollywood.[115]

Robert Clarke was again the hero as he battled the strange, wooden-faced little man who had designs upon our world and who turned men into zombies with a needle-thin ray from his bathyspherical space ship.

The Thing (from Another World) (RKO, 1951) was welcome proof that the bigger producers were in there pitching also. Howard Hawks put together a science-fiction film which proved to be a magnificent tour-de-force of suspense and horror, capably directed by Christian Nyby. The Thing was based on a story by John W. Campbell,

---

[113] "Civilization Ends—Again," Quick, Oct. 29, 1951, p. 56.

[114] Winthrop Sargeant, "Through the Interstellar Looking Glass, Life, May 21, 1951, pp. 127-128.

[115] Fabun, op. cit., p. 55

Jr., editor of one of the most adult of the science-fiction magazines, Astounding Science Fiction. The Thing was

> . . . a ferocious vegetable, 8 feet tall, delivered on a flying saucer from another world. It bleeds green, howls like an aggravated banshee, multiplies by dropping seeds into the earth. It thinks like Einstein, looks like Frankenstein's monster, and, like Dracula, thrives only on a diet of human blood.[116]
>
> Its tongue just perceptible in its cheek, the picture goes about describing the arrival of the Martian on our earth in quite a plausible manner.
>
> . . . .
>
> . . . this . . . mystery drama . . . is even livelier than the sort of thing that went on when Boris Karloff was lumbering around as Frankenstein's monster. It would be justifiable, I guess, to take small exception to the physical appearance of the Martian in this film. Although the scientist declares he's a kind of super-intellectual carrot, he doesn't look a lot different from most of the screen horrors that have gone before him.[117]

Comparison with Frankenstein's monster seemed inevitable, as indeed the Thing did resemble him in the few brief glimpses we were permitted. This off-staging was a wise decision, as it did much to heighten the dread and terror of the creature itself, which actually, as "played with dread anonymity by James Arness—was certainly less forbidding than the Frankenstein monster . . . to . . . whom the creature owed a very discernible resemblance."[118] Science-fiction fans

---

[116] "Cinema," Time, May 14, 1951, p. 110.

[117] "The Current Cinema," The New Yorker, May 12, 1951, p. 93.

[118] Nealon, op. cit., p. 107.

deplored the liberties taken with Campbell's original story, "Who Goes There?" but there was no denying that this science-horror movie was good box-office material as well as good, gripping cinema:

> . . . Hollywood realized it had laid a golden monster. Even before its initial run through was completed, The Thing had rung up over $2,000,000 and it had a big future ahead of it.[119]

> I was scared to death for a considerable portion of the running time by this Howard Hawks production. . . . The Thing falls, I guess, into the category of science-fiction, and it would seem to me that if the category continues to be as well treated as this there's going to be a bright motion-picture future for the stuff.
>
> . . . .
>
> . . . I think Christian Nyby, the director, is in for some high compliments for keeping the tension of the audience at a keen, awed pitch and for the convincing detail that keeps one's inclination to disbelief suspended until the lights go on.[120]

Briefly, the plot concerned the discovery of a flying saucer by a group of Air Force personnel and a few scientists (including a sweater-bulging secretary), stationed at a remote Antarctic outpost to keep a watch out for any Soviet shenanigans. The ship had been frozen in the ice for some time, and in an attempt to thaw it out with thermite, the exploring party destroys it; but they find its occupant, a huge, man-like creature, intact. They chop him out and take him back to the base, where he accidentally thaws out and begins raising havoc with people

---

[119] Fabun, op. cit., p. 53.

[120] Hollis Alpert, "SRL Goes to the Movies," Saturday Review of Literature, April 21, 1951, p. 28.

and sled dogs. He turns out to be a sentient vegetable, able to reproduce by dropping chunks of himself, such as a grisly hand torn off by the dogs, and with a thirst for human blood. The small group, headed by an Air Force Captain (Kenneth Tobey), try repeatedly to destroy the Thing, but to no avail. To add to their trouble, an idealistic scientist (Robert Cornthwaite) insists upon complicating things by wanting to preserve the monster for research, and tries to communicate with it, to his ultimate dismay. After all else fails, the Thing is finally cooked to death by electricity in a spine-chilling climax, and the earth is saved—for a while.

Next, 20th-Century Fox entered the scientifiction sweepstakes with The Day the Earth Stood Still (1951), a solid, well-made film with a message. Produced by Julian Blaustein and directed by Robert Wise, this film had everything—humor, suspense, terror, plenty of science-fiction gadgets for everybody (including a giant robot with a death ray, a sleek flying saucer, and a resurrection machine), a perhaps-too-baldly-stated moral,and for the intellectuals, there was an allegory of Christ.

> The Day the Earth Stood Still is a science-fiction thriller based on perhaps as happy an event as might be imagined in connection with a Flying Saucer. This particular saucer whirls to earth in Washington, D. C., where it disgorges not only a ghastly robot but also a man rather Lincolnesque in his beardless way, Klaatu (Michael Rennie), whose message to the warring world simply is that if its new atomic powers are used to disturb the peace of the other planets, they, with their advanced techniques, will blast the world off the face of the universe.

> This pacific suggestion is solemn enough, but the picture prefers to chase after comic possibilities and heads rapidly for the area of light entertainment. . . . The frustrations of an unworldly visitor incognito in Washington and among the disunities of the earth are worked for considerable mild amusement. . . .
>
> The story finally reverts to melodrama when Klaatu, to draw international attention to his message, neutralizes the world's electricity for a half hour. And after Klaatu has been trapped by the army and ostensibly killed, the robot retrieves the body and it is revived, scientifically, aboard the space ship. Klaatu pays his modest respects to the divine power over life and death, conceding that his resurrection is only temporary and of uncertain duration. But by this time the picture's fun has long been over, and its message has come to seem a mere afterthought to Hollywood showmanship.[121]

Five (Columbia, 1951) was a small independent production shot by former radio showman Arch Oboler on a miniscule budget, in an attempt to make a more "artistic" science-fiction film than Hollywood had come up with.

> *Five* . . . was shot . . . in the hills of Santa Monica but released through the regular channels of Columbia. *Five* is perhaps the purest example of the "socio-economic" or "socio-psychologic" science-fiction story. It was magnificently photographed, and incredibly well cast. It dealt with conflict between the last five persons on earth after an atomic cataclysm. Despite all the factors which should have made it the greatest picture of its type and time, *Five* had only mediocre success, and there were many science-fiction people who did not think it sufficiently exciting nor sufficiently scientific to classify as "true" science fiction.[122]

Newsweek concurred. They called it

> . . . an unusual melodrama with a potential gallop that is pulled up short in the stretch. . . . Unfortunately for the future of *Five*,

---

[121] "Movies," *Newsweek*, October 1, 1951, p. 90.

[122] Fabun, *op. cit.*, pp. 57-58.

its best portions are the camera's silent comment on blasted, deserted cities, empty highways, and villages. There is little about the survivors and what happens to them that deserves special attention.

. . . .

In tackling his timely theme Oboler, surprisingly, provides little that is either significant or dramatic in the physical or moral conflicts that beset these people whose Genesis begins with "the day after tomorrow." Both his dialogue (with poetic flights) and his direction are pedestrian in the light of the film's artistic pretensions. His players—comparative unknowns chosen to match a shoestring budget of $75,000—share with Oboler the faint praise of good intentions.[123]

Fox couldn't quit while they were ahead. The same year as The Day the Earth Stood Still they released I'll Never Forget You (1951), a pseudo-time-travel story, based on the play Berkeley Square by John L. Balderston.

I'll Never Forget You is a remake of Berkeley Square, with Tyrone Power in the role played originally by the late Leslie Howard. In the new version, Power is a U. S. atomic scientist suffering from acute Anglophobia with historical complications. His yearning to live in 18th century England thrusts him mysteriously one evening into the Technicolored London of his ancestors.

Playwright John Balderston's old trick with time—turning his hero's hindsight into prophetic genius—is still a neat trick, and the new movie has some fun with it. But Actor Power lacks Actor Howard's charm and talent, and his inter-century romance with Ann Blyth (who turns up at the end in a twentieth century reincarnation) makes something gooey and adolescent out of what once seemed hauntingly otherworldly. The picture may give moviegoers a yen to go back in time themselves, if only to 1933, when Leslie Howard was starring in Berkeley Square.[124]

---

[123]"Movies," Newsweek, May 7, 1951, p. 90.

[124]"Cinema," Time, January 14, 1952, p. 92.

George Pal, never one to rest on his laurels, had been planning something big ever since the overwhelming success of Destination Moon in 1950. He found what he was looking for in When Worlds Collide, a 1932 novel by Edwin Balmer and Philip Wylie. Pal bought it from Paramount (who had intended to do it as a De Mille spectacle years ago, but abandoned it as "too fantastic"), dusted it off, brought it up to date, and put all of his considerable special effects talent to work on it. Paramount, after observing the success of science-fiction films all around them, bought the book back, and Pal produced it for them instead of independently, as he had Destination Moon.[125]

> When Worlds Collide was George Pal's second big-time entry in the science-fiction field. Destination Moon had been a winner, all the way around, but there was a general feeling that it lacked "story." . . . When Worlds Collide was intended to remedy this deficiency. It was a true Hollywood spectacle, with all the charm that word has had for movie audiences since the days of Ben Hur, and it had "romantic interest."[126]

Once again, Pal strove for technical accuracy, in order to make the fantastic believable: "Leading U. S. scientists were frequent visitors to the set . . ."[127] It was good, and it was successful at the box office, making over a million in 1951:

> When Worlds Collide is better than . . . its predecessors. For comparison one has to hark back to Korda's Shape of Things to

---

[125]Richardson, op. cit., pp. 96-97.

[126]Fabun, op. cit., p. 56.

[127]"Escape to the Stars," Parade, August 5, 1951, p. 22.

Come, and even in this comparison Worlds doesn't suffer. It is an adult and well-made movie, beautifully developing the suspense of its theme, and at the same time neatly skirting both the sensationalism and the sentimentality which could easily have marred it.[128]

The story line is a simple one; it tells of the near approach of another star and its planet, the disruption their gravitational fields cause on earth, and the construction and launching of a rocket that enables a group of humans to escape earth before the s star crashes into it. A reasonably strong romantic story could be developed within this setting, and George Pal made the most of it. Spectacular scenes of earthly cataclysm, staged and filmed partly in miniature and with considerable ingenuity, provided sufficient come-on for those members of the audience who hadn't realized there were other planets until now.[129]

Flight to Mars (Monogram, 1951) was another one of the "cheapies": a Cinecolored voyage to a Mars peopled with very human-looking girls in short skirts.

Robert L. Lippert, not to be outdone, was still in there pitching and decided it was about time to do The Lost World again. So he did, and called it The Lost Continent (1951). Cesar Romero starred as the head of a U. S. Army party on a mission to retrive a runaway rocket, which brings them to a forgotten plateau "where life, animal and vegetable, is as it was millions of years ago. An earthquake helps the party escape from prehistoric monsters."[130] Before 1951 was quite over, Lippert squeezed one more film in: Unknown World, in which

---

[128] Al Hine, "Pagans and Planets," Holiday, November, 1951, pp. 24-25.

[129] Fabun, loc. cit.

[130] "Films Incorporated Recreational 1956-1957 Catalog," p. 61.

Bruce Kellogg and a few other people delved into the center of the earth in a mechanical mole machine.

Apparently they caused a disturbance down there, for Superman, who had returned to make another serial, had trouble with underground invaders in *Superman and the Mole Men* (1951). This serial was the closest to "legitimate science-fiction" that Superman ever got. Other serials of 1951 included: *Captain Video*, transplanted from television; *Flying Disc Man from Mars*, and *The Mysterious Island*, Sam Katzman's working over of Verne's novel.

Although this new renaissance of science-fiction films was largely monopolized by the United States, there were two very interesting pictures produced overseas, one in Russia and one in Czechoslovakia. The Czech film *Krakatit* was an adaptation of

> . . . the prophetic 1920 novel by the imaginative and inspired Czech idealist, Karel Capek, who also wrote *R. U. R.* and *World of the Insects*. Twenty-five years before the atomic age, Capek envisioned with uncanny accuracy the theory of atomic explosion when he wrote *Krakatit*. Capek sought, through his hero, Prokop, the scientist who discovers the explosive "Krakatit," to help men find their way towards a sane solution to the dangers inherent in atomic warfare. The feverish dreams of Prokop, oscillating between the real and the unreal, the present and the future, are translated into cinematic and musical terms which express the whole scale of his psychological changes.[131]

The Russian film was a crude and shocking propaganda film, never intended for American distribution, but of which *Life* magazine

---

[131]"Brandon International Film Classics Rental Catalog" (No. 25), 1957, p. 28.

managed to obtain a print:

> In newspaper editorials, cartoons and even history books, Soviet propagandists picture the U. S. as a whisky-soaked land run by a gangster group of businessmen, politicians, generals and clergymen, all in cahoots. Although most Americans realize that this is the official Communist line, few know to what extremes Red propagandists go. The luridness of their characterization is shockingly dramatized by a motion picture called Silvery Dust, now being shown in Russia and satellite countries.
>
> The film, a print of which was obtained by LIFE from a European source, is built around a fictitious American scientist who has developed a ghastly radioactive substance capable of wiping out vast areas of the world. He needs human guinea pigs to prove the deadliness of his dust. As he tries to round up some victims, two rival tycoons—with a wicked general and a Nazi scientist as go-betweens—battle for control of the formula. The wild and wooly plot includes false arrests, kicking a Negro maid, a suborned complaint against her son and an attempted lynching, all of which, the film implies, are everyday occurrences in the U. S. Crude as this may seem to Americans—and however much it may puzzle some Russians who recall Kremlin pronouncements on the feasibility of "coexistence"—the film could well be effective propaganda for most iron curtain moviegoers who have no way of knowing what a monstrous fraud they are watching.[132]

The year 1952 was a disappointing one for science-fiction film fans. Only a few scientifilms were produced, and some "borderline cases," such as Britain's Breaking the Sound Barrier (London Films, 1952), "a brilliant British melodrama based on the unearthly and scarifying harsh hiss of the jet airplane engines as they gradually approach and surpass the speed of sound."[133]

The Man in the White Suit (Rank, 1952), was another excellent

---

[132] "Red's-Eye View of U. S.," Life, October 11, 1954, p. 83.

[133] "Movies," Newsweek, December 1, 1952, p. 82.

British film, primarily a comedy, but with some pointed social comment:

> The Man in the White Suit spins a colorful yarn out of whole cloth about a research chemist (Alec Guiness) who invents an artificial fabric that will never stain or wear out. The result is top-grade movie material with the quality of good British woolen, the frothiness of fine French lace.[134]

Two serials, Dick Tracy vs. The Phantom Empire (Republic, 1952) and Radar Men from the Moon (Republic, 1952) appeared that year, and a little film called Red Planet Mars (United Artists, 1952) proved to be something of a "sleeper" to science-fiction fans. The story was interesting, "with a bit more meat to the plot than most of this type,"[135] it was capably directed and acted by Andrea King, Peter Graves and a few others, and was surprisingly "adult" for such a low-budget picture. The entire film took place on earth, and not one monstrous Martian menaced not one fair maiden. The story concerns a scientist who attempts to communicate with the planet Mars and finally succeeds in doing so—or so he believes, setting in motion a thrilling chain of events that threatens the safety of the entire world, and ultimately ends in a pseudo-religious climax in which Soviet Russia is overthrown and converted to Christianity and world peace is attained.

134"Cinema," Time, April 14, 1952, p. 108.

135Steven H. Scheuer, TV Movie Almanac and Ratings, 1958 and 1959 (New York: Bantam Books, 1958), p. 171.

But 1953 brought the deluge! Apparently having got their second wind, moviemakers both here and abroad produced a total of 27 features, documentaries, serials and shorts dealing with science-fiction. This was nine more than 1951's previously unequalled total of 18.[136]

Abbott and Costello started the ball rolling once again, with Abbott and Costello Go to Mars (Universal, 1953). Only they didn't go to Mars—they wound up instead on a planet inhabited by Miss Universe Contest Beauties, with Mari Blanchard as their queen. After a series of ridiculous escapades on earth, involving gangsters, scientists, flying saucers and a runaway rocket ship which roars through the Holland Tunnel, the two blast off for Mars, but land on Venus, where more slapstick awaits them.[137]

Invasion, U. S. A. (Columbia, 1953) was, according to Time,

> . . . a shoddy little shocker that combines a futuristic theme with old-hat moviemaking. A quintet of characters in a Manhattan bar hears the news that the U.S.S.R. is atom-bombing the United States. In the ensuing carnage, the quintet—a tractor manufacturer (Robert Bice), a rancher (Erik Blythe), a Congressman (Wade Crosby), a TV reporter (Gerald Mohr) and a beautiful blonde (Peggie Castle)—are killed off.
>
> A trick ending reveals all the preceding events to have been nothing more than a pipe dream resulting from mass hypnosis induced by a mysterious stranger (Dan O'Herlihy) as a plea for preparedness. To go with this stock plot is a good deal of stock

---

[136] See Appendix, Table II, p. 177.

[137] "United World Films, Inc. 1959 Catalog," p. 38.

> newsreel footage of atomic explosions and battle scenes. The newsreel shots give the picture what little authenticity it has.[138]

France contributed Alerte au Sud (Alert in the South) (1953), directed by Jean Devaivre, which told of happenings when, "From the heart of the Sahara, a ray which paralyzes or kills" is detected.[139] Germany re-made Alraune for the third time, this time starring Hildegarde Neff and Erich von Stroheim, and directed by A. M. Rabenalt:

> It is the story of a girl conceived by artificial insemination who is devoid of love and compassion and is completely the creature of the man who dreamed her up. Gradually, however, she frees herself from his bondage, but in the process the men in her wake wilt like so many flowers.[140]

The Magnetic Monster (United Artists, 1953) brought Curt Siodmak back to the science-fiction film scene once more, to direct and co-author (with producer Ivan Tors) a "modest but exciting sample of science fiction."[141]

> The monster in this crackling mixture of science and fiction is a newly discovered radioactive element that grows so fast and has such a powerful magnetic field that it threatens to destroy the earth. In the nick of time, the substance is destroyed by being fed an outsize dose of electric power.

---

[138] "Cinema," Time, February 16, 1953, p. 106.

[139] Michel Laclos, op. cit., p. xxxii.

[140] Manfred George, "Hildegarde Neff," Films in Review, November, 1955, p. 447.

[141] "Movies," Newsweek, March 2, 1953, p. 91.

> Directed at a breakneck pace by Co-Author Curt Siodmak, *The Magnetic Monster* is crisply acted by Richard Carlson and King Donovan, as scientists combatting the radioactive threat. . . . The whole thing is up to the minute and quasi-scientifically hair-raising.[142]

The picture was made very cheaply, and seemed to help prove that it was just as easy to make good low-budget films as bad ones. To help cut corners, the whole climax was lifted from an earlier German film, *Gold*, and used as the atom-smashing conclusion.[143]

The Beast from 20,000 Fathoms (Warner Bros., 1953) brought to the screen the biggest city-destroyer since King Kong, a gigantic prehistoric lizard called a "rhedosaurus," "which gets to Coney Island after being dislodged by an Arctic atom-bomb test from a million-year hibernation."[144] Based on a *Saturday Evening Post* short story by Ray Bradbury which later appeared under the title "The Foghorn," the Beast was directed by Eugene Lourie, and featured some excellent effects by Ray Harryhausen.

> *The Beast from 20,000 Fathoms* has a climactic sequence that seems to have been made to order for 3-D: a prehistoric monster tangled up in a Coney Island roller coaster. . . . The picture has a few scary moments when the special-effects men, unhampered by antediluvian human dramatics, let the rhedosaurus run loose in Manhattan, knocking over buildings, crushing automobiles underfoot, swallowing policemen.[145]

---

[142] "Cinema," *Time*, February 16, 1953, pp. 104, 106.

[143] *Supra*, p. 49.

[144] "Cinema," *Time*, June 22, 1953, p. 88.

[145] *Ibid*.

In the original story, Bradbury's beast contented itself with knocking over an irritating lighthouse, but in the film this was only one of his many malicious pranks. This picture, although no one realized it at the time, was the turning point in the kind of science-fiction pictures being made. From then on, more and more giant creatures of every kind began to appear, leaving behind the more conventional stories of voyages into space and smaller, more scientific menaces.

Invaders from Mars (20th Century-Fox, 1953) brought to earth a fantastic horde of seven-foot-tall green Martians, telepathically directed by a hideous tentacled brain in a glass globe. They set up underground headquarters underground, and the film deals with the efforts of a small boy (Jimmy Hunt) to save his parents from their clutches. Capturing adults, the Martians surgically implant a device in their skulls which turns them into zombies, forced to obey the will of the Brain. This color production was designed and directed by the late William Cameron Menzies, who had directed Things to Come, and by all rights, it should have been a good film. But somehow, Menzies came up with nothing but a sterile collection of clichés and wooden acting, and the ending—as in Invasion, U.S.A.—discloses that it was all a little boy's dream![146]

---

[146]Only one magazine deigned to review this film (National Parent Teacher, 47:37, June, 1953). How the mighty Menzies had fallen!

By this time, the new 3-D craze that had hit the movies, beginning with Arch Oboler's Bwana Devil, a jungle picture, was being considered by a few producers as the perfect medium in which to portray science-fiction. What could be better than meteors, monsters and mad scientists popping out at you from the screen? Fortunately, the first entry into the field was somewhat restrained, and its 3-D effects well chosen to enhance the chilling effect of the picture. It came from Outer Space (Universal, 1953) featured a giant, multi-faceted space globe that roared into the audience, a landslide that kept them dodging, and the world's first "subjective monster shots":

> It Came from Outer Space is one of those modestly budgeted, neatly tooled little thrillers that Hollywood turns out without fanfare from time to time. Based on a story by Ray Bradbury,[147] it is a crisp combination of shocker and sociological comment. It tells of a Martian space ship that lands in the Arizona desert and of the chaos the visitors from outer space cause before they depart.
>
> As readers of Bradbury's science fiction will guess, his Martians are no mere bogeymen.[148] They are highly intelligent, peace-loving beings who happen to land on the earth by error while on their way to another planet. All they want is to repair their space ship and move on. They do not want to encounter any human

---

[147] William Alland once allowed Ray Bradbury to concoct something called a "treatment" . . . but science-fiction's most gifted author was not permitted to touch the actual shooting script. That delicate work was handed to one Harry Essex, a Hollywood pro, who by his own admission knew little of s-f. That the picture (It Came From Outer Space) turned out reasonably well is largely due to Essex' faithfulness to the Bradbury original. Hollis Alpert and Charles Beaumont, "The Horror of It all," Playboy, March, 1959, p. 87.

[148] The publicity department cooked up the fancy name of "Xenomorphs" for them.

> beings, who have not reached the advanced stage of civilization essential to such a meeting. The Martians' appearance—the face is a bare, embryo-like mass with a looming eye in the center—would alarm the humans, and, as one of the characters in the picture says, "What men don't understand, they destroy." Thus, in order to go about repairing their ship, the Martians disguise themselves as humans, adopting the shapes of certain men and women in the vicinity.
>
> Except for a couple of quick, vivid shots the Martians are not seen on the screen. But the story is occasionally told from the Martian point of view, as seen through a shimmering eyelike bubble of film. Director Jack Arnold has made good use of the barren brooding desert expanses with their lonely, unreal look of another world, and the picture is well acted, particularly by Richard Carlson, as a mystically inclined astronomer.[149]

Cat-Women of the Moon (Astor, 1953) was also photographed in 3-D and starred Victor Jory, Marie Windsor and Sonny Tufts. It was "about earth explorers on the moon. There, says producer Al Zimbalist, they find 'ugly-looking things like giant spiders with four eyes, and they blow poisonous fumes.' "[150]

Donovan's Brain (United Artists, 1953), written and directed by Felix Feist, was a re-make of the novel of the same name by Curt Siodmak. The 1944 version was called The Lady and the Monster, and turned out better, in spite of its title, than the 1953 version:

> Lew Ayres adds a false dignity to a "science" thriller of the comic-book variety. A young California scientist, who has had great success in keeping animal tissue alive, steals the brain of a ruthless tycoon who has been killed in a railroad accident and through laboratory mumbo jumbo keeps it alive. Scenes intended

---

[149] "Cinema," Time, July 6, 1953, p. 86.

[150] "Bloodstream Green," Time, Oct. 19, 1953, p. 112.

to be menacing or weird are distasteful instead.[151]

Project M-7 (Universal, 1953) was a British-made "science-fiction ripper, directed by Anthony Asquith, which attempts to capitalize on the Communist infiltration of the leading English drafting rooms."[152] A young scientist is developing a plane that will fly at fantastic speeds (3 times the speed of sound), and one of his buddies is a Commie spy. A routine spy melodrama, this film proved that "All that glitters is not gold, and everything that wears a space helmet is not thereby fascinating."[153]

Robert L. Lippert released two in 1953, Project Moonbase, written by Robert A. Heinlein and Jack Seaman, and Spaceways, starring Howard Duff and Eva Bartok. And they were accompanied by several other low-low budget thrillers, which did nothing to improve science-fiction's reputation with moviegoers: The Forty-Ninth Man (Columbia, 1953), The Neanderthal Man (United Artists, 1953), Phantom from Space (United Artists, 1953), Robot Monster (Astor, 1953), Run for the Hills (Realart, 1953), Sword of Venus (RKO, 1953) and a new Arch Oboler production, The Twonky (United Artists, 1953), taken from a short story by the late Henry Kuttner about a piece of

---

[151] "Motion Picture Previews," National Parent Teacher, December, 1953, p. 153.

[152] "Movies," Newsweek, January 4, 1954, p. 61.

[153] Ibid.

furniture from the future that goes haywire in a modern house. From Britain came The Four-Sided Triangle (Astor, 1953), starring Barbara Payton and based on the delightful novel by William F. Temple about a man who invents a machine that duplicates anything, and finds himself with two identical sweethearts!

Canadian Mounties vs. Atomic Invaders (Republic, 1953), Zombies of the Stratosphere (Republic, 1953) and The Lost Planet (Columbia, 1953) were entries in the serial division, the last named being Sam Katzman's latest, all about a new planet, Ergo, and filled with spark-spewing space ships, "mind-monitors," and a "cosmic cannon."[154] The Conquered Planet was a Dutch short, produced and directed by Hans Van Gelder and Martin Toonder, and Flying Saucers was an excellent German documentary on the subject.

It was up to George Pal, science-fiction veteran by this time, to top them all in 1953. For his most ambitious production to date, he reached back into science-fiction history and dusted off H. G. Wells' classic 1898 novel of invasion from Mars, The War of the Worlds. In an article in Astounding Science Fiction, Mr. Pal explained how he conceived the idea of filming the Wells novel:

> War of the Worlds was on my agenda of future projects almost since the day I arrived at Paramount Studio two and one half years ago after producing my first science-fiction venture, Destination Moon for Eagle-Lion release.
>
> Paramount had owned the Wells story for some twenty-six years but no producer had ever tackled it, although it had been

---

[154] "Meet Jungle Sam," Life, March 23, 1953, pp. 80-81.

discussed several times.[155] But now with the big vogue for films of a science-fiction nature it seemed a logical choice.

So it was natural that I selected it as one of my first story properties for future production.

I was stimulated by the problems it posed. Although written fifty-six years ago, in many respects it had withstood the advances of time remarkably well and remained today an exciting and visionary story of the future.

It offered me my greatest challenge to date in figuring out how to film the Martian machines, their heat and disintegration rays and the destruction and chaos they cause when they invade Earth.

It ended up by being my most costly picture to date, $2,000,000, as contrasted with $586,000 for Destination Moon, and $963,000 for When Worlds Collide.

It also took the longest period of time to make. More than six months of special-effects work plus an additional two months for optical effects were needed after our regular shooting schedule with the cast was concluded; work with the cast took forty days at the studio and on location in Arizona.[156]

Pal worked long and hard on this Technicolored spectacle and was rewarded by the comments of many science-fiction fans as well as average moviegoers, who voted it the best science-fiction film ever made. And that, from fault-picking science-fiction fans, was high praise!

---

[155] Jay Leyda (ed.), "The Work of Eisenstein," Film Form and The Film Sense (New York: Meridian Books, 1957), p. 223. When Eisenstein signed the contract with Paramount in Paris, Jesse Lasky proposed to him the H. G. Wells novel, but the project was soon dropped as too costly.

[156] George Pal, "Filming War of the Worlds," Astounding Science Fiction, October, 1953, pp. 100-101.

> The tremendous pyrotechnics of this film add incalculably to its over-all impact. For the first time, force screens are depicted on the screen. Also present are antigravity ships with realistic heat rays. The moviegoer is carried from one marvel to the next. The slight attempts at love interest are merely irksome interludes and one is happy to find a convincingly contrived, truly alien-looking Martian interrupting such frivolity. The destruction of Los Angeles is most impressive.
>
> Though some modifications were necessary to modernize this Wells story, the final result was excellent. . . . There is no question that The War of the Worlds is a landmark in the production of science-fiction films.[157]

No one seemed to object that the story was brought up to date and the locale shifted from Britain to Los Angeles and Southern California. Orson Welles' panic-provoking radio version of War of the Worlds in 1938 had also helped to pre-sell the story, as many people had heard the broadcast, or at least heard of it. "Thanks to wonderfully imaginative animation work and some fine, eerie sound effects," wrote critic Arthur Knight in The Saturday Review, "this filmic invasion is something to see."[158]

April 1, 2000 started off 1954's crop of science-fiction films.

---

[157]"The War of the Worlds," Science-Fiction Plus, August, 1953, p. 67.

[158]Arthur Knight, "SR Goes to the Movies," The Saturday Review, September 12, 1953, p. 47. In 1956 senior students at USC produced an amusing short in 16mm called The Red Menace, which told of a rebellious coke machine, which, with a personality all its own, refused to produce cokes. Sound tracks obtained from Paramount which had been used in War of the Worlds provided a fascinating accompaniment to the machine's obtuseness, until it finally gave forth —a bottle of beer!

This was an amusing Austrian satire, produced in Vienna and starring Curt Jurgens.

> This imaginative political satire, made in Vienna, is a plea for an Austrian peace treaty. It is also an epic potpourri of historical pageantry, indigenous operetta music, and Austria's national art treasures.
>
> It opens, 46 years hence, with a new Austrian president abruptly and defiantly announcing his country's freedom from the four-power occupation. The population's joy is not altogether unconfined, for there is concern over what the Global Union, a kind of super UN that keeps peace on this planet, may do.
>
> From out of the stratosphere, in weird rocket aircraft, descends upon Vienna the World Security Council, accompanied by its own police force equipped with appropriately fearsome weapons. Austria is charged with aggression.
>
> Mobilizing all the resources of stage, screen, radio and TV, the Austrian president defends his country by summoning up the military and cultural glories of the Austrian past. . . .
>
> The six permanent members of the World Security Council are rather interesting from the political point of view. They are representatives of North America, South America, Europe, Africa, Asia, and what is called "the Moslem Union." Four are individually characterized. The South American, an alluring brunette, is a child of nature. (She falls for Austria's bachelor president and helps him win the day.) . . .
>
> The costumes of the World Security Council's police are straight out of science-fiction. They wear feline-appearing helmets and carry death-ray and "search-ray" guns. The latter render walls, closets, desks, etc., transparent. A bit of farce pops occasionally, as when the captain of the police force faints at the sight of blood _in a movie_. "I could never kill—with my bare hands," he cries, in horror.
>
> The clothes of the diplomats and of the Austrian population in the year 2000 are not noteworthy for style innovations, though those of the lady politicos have a somewhat futuristic flair. The cleverest outfits are the glistening antennae headpieces and wrist-watch microphones worn by radio commentators and TV

cameramen.

The unearthing of a long-forgotten agreement signed by Roosevelt, Churchill and Stalin guaranteeing Austria's eventual freedom is rather awkwardly contrived, and the film's end is a bit mawkish.[159]

Avant le Deluge (Before the Deluge) (1954) was made in France, and science-fiction writer Alan E. Nourse produced a fascinating science-fiction short, Born of Man and Woman, based on the short story by his fellow science-fiction writer, Richard Matheson. The Diamond Wizard (1954) was filmed in Britain, directed by and starring Dennis O'Keefe, and Immediate Disaster or A Visitor from Venus was a TV film starring Patricia Neal and Helmut Dantine, released theatrically in England and Australia.

Universal-International came up with a box-office bombshell in The Creature from the Black Lagoon (1954). Producer William Alland and make-up artist Wally Westmore and his staff dreamed up a new kind of monster, a fearsome creature called "The Gill Man," part human, part fish and part frog. Jack Arnold directed, veteran science-fiction film star Richard Carlson played in it, along with Julia Adams, Richard Denning, Whit Bissell and featuring Ben Chapman as "the Creature." How this $3,000,000 monster came to be is told in affectionate detail by his creator in a Collier's article by Joseph Laitin:

---

[159] N. Hope Wilson, "Film Reviews," Films in Review, March, 1954, pp. 142-143.

> Producer Alland phoned and said he was toying with a movie based on an old South American legend that somewhere up the Amazon still existed a man from the Devonian age, part human, part alligator, part turtle. "If you can deliver a monster like that, we'll write a script around it," said Alland [to Westmore]. The Gill Man posed several unprecedented problems for the laboratory team. He had to be able to swim freely and effectively, walk on land, breathe through pulsating gills—and, most important, not look like a man in a rubber suit. "We gave him two arms with crab claws," says Westmore, "and we first had him with a tail and a built-in engine to operate it, so he could swish a man off his feet. But that interefered with his swimming, so we cut it out. His chin, obviously, we took from the frog. His mouth? Look at any fish. The pulsating gills covered up the actor's ears—always a problem—and supplied a menacing type of movement. The head was finally shaped up on an old bust of Ann Sheridan—the only one we had with a neck.[160]

No one took the Gill Man very seriously, but he became very popular, despite some critical disapproval. His underwater 3-D antics were very suspenseful and he was properly ferocious and menacing.

> You're not supposed to believe The Creature from the Black Lagoon, but you can if you want to; and if you approach it with your tongue in cheek and your 3-D glasses firmly planted you'll have a good scare and maybe even a laugh.[161]

Gog (United Artists, 1954) was the latest brainstorm of producer-writer Ivan Tors who made The Magnetic Monster. It starred Richard Egan, Constance Dowling and Herbert Marshall, and was directed and edited by Herbert L. Strock. "Gog" was the name given to

> . . . a tidy, legless little robot with five arms, a beer-barrel belly, and a head like a chrome-plated grapefruit with a gleaming

---

[160] Joseph Laitin, "Monsters Made to Order," Collier's, December 10, 1954, p. 53.

[161] Philip T. Hartung, "The Screen," Commonweal, May 14,

red aerial on top. Gog is married—or something—to another robot named Magog, and they both work in a highly secret space-research institute hidden somewhere underneath the great American desert, which Herbert Marshall runs for the government.[162]

The great thing about science fiction is that it imposes no limitation whatever on the imagination . . . Gog takes full advantage of this, and incorporates in one film many of the best of the current sci-fic gimmicks.

Gog's basic plot concerns an attempt . . . to solve the problems inherent in the creation and launching of a man-made satellite, which, revolving around the earth, would serve as both an omnipresent eye and a weapon base. Gog's elucidation of some of these problems is quite interesting, even though far from comprehensive, and never wholly convincing.

The plot complications consist of the sabotage of the satellite project by an unseen, and unnamed, enemy, and the elimination of top scientists in really novel ways. Two are frozen to death in their own low-temperature experimental chamber; one is killed by radioactive poisoning; two by centrifugal force; one by supersonic vibrations; and two by robots controlled by a huge electronic mathematical calculator. Another killing is almost effected by refracted isolation.

Herbert Marshall, as the head of the satellite project, is nothing to write home about, nor is anyone else in the cast. But William Ferrari's art work is ingenious and occasionally imaginative. . . .[163]

The Atomic Kid (Republic, 1954) was a zany science-fiction comedy about a man (Mickey Rooney) who becomes radioactive from an atomic blast, and Killers from Space (RKO, 1954) pitted Peter Graves

---

1954, p. 145.

[162] "Cinema," Time, July 19, 1954, pp. 78-79.

[163] In 3-D and Eastman Color. Paul Heller, "Film Reviews," Films in Review, August-September, 1954, pp. 368-369.

against space men with ping-pong balls for eyes.

Monster from the Ocean Floor (Lippert, 1954) was a modern version of the Perseus-Andromeda legend, set in Mexico and directed by Wyatt Ordung.

> The story concerns a beautiful American artist who is to be offered as a sacrifice to their Gods by natives in an attempt to ward off a sea monster that has been terrorizing the swimmers near a Mexican village. She is rescued when the hero, a biologist, kills the beast in a savage underwater encounter.[164]

Riders to the Stars (United Artists, 1954) was yet another color space thriller from the Tors-Carlson-Siodmak group.

> Once again Curt Siodmak . . . has scripted another stirring scientifilm. Riders to the Stars promises to be an even more memorable treat than his classic FP 1 or the later TransAtlantic Tunnel, or recent hit, Magnetic Monster. Like the latter, the picture has been produced by Ivan Tors, and the pair of men make a winning team. With excellent actor Richard Carlson, himself an early devotee of stf, completing the triangle, a top product is assured.[165]

> Riders to the Stars is an oater of the ionosphere. The hero (William Lundigan) is a rocket jockey, the first man ever to ride a guided missile through the wide open spaces beyond earth's atmosphere. The heroine (Martha Hyer) is a "space-medicine girl" who "dreams of flying almost every night." The rocket man is told by his double-dome dad (Herbert Marshall), a rocket scientist, to go and catch a meteorite. He does this, 80 miles above the earth, with the help of the most startling invention since the Sky Hook—the "Meteor Scoop." Details are not disclosed (presumably they are not yet known to the Russians), but the principle is evident: the rocket has a lower lip that drops down at the strategic

---

164. "Films Incorporated Recreational 1956-1957 Catalog," p. 62.

165. Forrest J Ackerman, "Scientifilm Parade," Spaceway, April, 1954, p. 89.

time and the meteorite just pops in like an interstellar sourball.[166]

The Rocket Man (20th Century-Fox) turned out to be an amusing little science-fantasy starring Charles Coburn, Anne Francis, John Agar, Spring Byington and George "Foghorn" Winslow, "who turned an American town upside down! The story, with a small-town locale, is given a modern twist by the antics of young Winslow, who uses a magic-ray gun given him by an ephemeral space man, who instructs him in its use."[167]

The Snow Creature (United Artists, 1954) attempted to capitalize on the legend of the "Abominable Snowman" of the Himalayas; Tobor the Great (Republic, 1954) was a weird-looking robot who made friends with a little boy and spent most of his time smashing enemy agents and things,[168] and Allied Artists released World for Ransom, starring Dan Duryea, Gene Lockhart and Arthur Shields, and Target—Earth!, starring Richard Denning and Virginia Grey. Produced by Herman Cohen, this picture was based on "Deadly City," a short story by Ivor Jorgenson (Paul W. Fairman):

> The basic film-plot of Target—Earth! resembles, in its opening reels, the earlier Atomigeddon sleeper, Five, conceived by Arch Oboler. A handful of characters meet in an empty city.

---

[166]"Cinema," Time, March 15, 1952, p. 106.

[167]"Films Incorporated Catalog," op. cit., p. 46.

[168]Forrest J Ackerman, "Scientifilm Parade," Spaceway, April, 1955, p. 66.

At first they wake, one by one, from sleeping pills, drunken stupor, etc., in various parts of the silent city. None can conceive of an explanation for the evacuation of a population of millions in a matter of 8 hours. Desperately searching for another human being, one by one they come upon each other and band together against the unknown.

The unknown comes at last in the form of a giant shadow projected briefly on the side of a skyscraper.

The menace is finally revealed to be an alien automaton, a metal man who is the vanguard of an invasion—an invasion from Venus. The Venusian robot can kill via a destructive ray similar to that of Gort in The Day the Earth Stood Still.[169]

Them! (Warner Bros., 1954) was a little more expensive production than the preceding few mentioned above, and starred James Whitmore, Edmund Gwenn, James Arness and Joan Weldon. The picture continued the trend begun by The Beast from 20,000 Fathoms, namely, having a giant something-or-other menace the earth. In this case, it was giant, mutated ants. But the picture was well done, and truly horrifying:

> . . . For many, if not most devotees of science fiction, the great thing is not to make the fantastic seem superfantastic but to give it the strong illusion of reality. Judged by that standard, this is a right little fright of a picture. Its opening scenes are commonplace; its clear, realistic photography is in prosaic black and white; its characters have an everyday credibility. And so the way is prepared to make its ghastly developments more or less believable.[170]

The terrifying creatures panic nearby desert towns as they

---

[169] Ackerman, op. cit., pp. 65-66.

[170] "Movies," Newsweek, June 7, 1954, p. 56.

forage for food, killing the hapless humans who happen to cross their paths with gigantic doses of formic acid. Mutated by the 1945 atom-bomb tests, the ants are tracked down by a pair of entomologists, Edmund Gwenn and Joan Weldon. Together with police sergeant James Whitmore and FBI agent James Arness, they exterminate all but the queens, who escape to the storm drains of Los Angeles, where they are hunted down in a gripping, horrifying climax. Intelligently directed by Gordon Douglas, there were many grisly little touches that helped to set and maintain the mood of terror throughout the film, despite a lot of talk. One such was the scene in which the little party, observing one of the giant ant hills in the desert from a helicopter, watch with horror as a huge ant pokes his head out, carrying a human rib-cage in his mandibles!

> The acting is rather more believable in Them than in Gog, but then so are the monsters. Hairy brutes they are, with just that expression of chinless, bulge-eyed evil that Peter Lorre has been trying all these years to achieve.[171]

As if in answer to this challenge, Peter Lorre turned up, along with a very distinguished cast, in the science-fiction spectacle of the year: Walt Disney's elaborate production, in CinemaScope and Technicolor, of Jules Verne's Twenty Thousand Leagues Under the Sea. Long awaited by science-fiction and Disney fans alike, this colorful film proved to be a treat in every way. Action, adventure, terror,

---

[171]"Cinema," Time, July 19, 1954, p. 79.

humor, songs and music—all were there, as Verne's novel of undersea adventure came to life on the screen in the inimitable Disney fashion. Directed by Richard Fleischer, spectacle after spectacle delighted the eye: the wonderful submarine of Captain Nemo (fascinatingly played by James Mason), the Nautilus; magnificent underwater scenes; the "atomic" power-room of the sub; the hair-raising fight with the giant squid—one of the most realistic of all screen monsters and the final, cataclysmic explosion of Nemo's island. Kirk Douglas and Paul Luka rounded out the cast. This was the first science-fiction film in CinemaScope, and showed how well adapted the wide screen was for science-fiction.

> . . . Walt Disney was well advised to try his hand at this exciting science-fiction story of Jules Verne's. How modern it is! And how technically inventive Disney and his aides have been in making this film about it!
>
> In their film the wonderful submarine, the Nautilus, is exactly as Verne imaginatively described it more than eighty years ago. It was run by a kind of atomic power, and was operated entirely by electricity.
>
> . . . .
>
> An appropriate air of mystery is maintained throughout this excellent film largely by virtue of the colorful and historically interesting sets of John Meehan. . . . And the expert CinemaScope photography of Cameraman Till Gabbani keeps every scene visually alive. His underwater shots on the sea floor, especially of the burial scene, are full of natural beauty—and all too few.
>
> The very complex character of Captain Nemo is very convincingly portrayed by James Mason, who is well-equipped to make plausible Nemo's almost Nietzchean hatred for human stupidity and cruelty, and his simultaneous and idealistic reverence for his own

world of the deep. In the end, of course, he inevitably destroys himself. As the sympathetic Professor Arronax (woodenly played by Paul Lukas) says, Nemo was ahead of his time. . . .[172]

In 1955, the monsters were upon us! The Beast with 1,000,000 Eyes (American Releasing Corporation, 1955) was a "weirdie from another planet which can project itself into the body of all but intelligent human beings."[173] This creature, which was seen only briefly in the film, was the initial creation of a new special-effects talent and monster maker, artist Paul Blaisdell. His monsters were to appear with ever-increasing frequency during the next few years.

The Creature with the Atom Brain (Columbia, 1955) proved that old Jungle Sam Katzman was still with us, this time utilizing the talents of Curt Siodmak, in a story about atomic zombies with the strength of ten men. Apparently the Katzman-Siodmak team didn't click:

> The Creature with the Atom Brain is a poor man's Donovan's Brain, jazzed up to meet current standards. Curt Siodmak is responsible, and we ought to be understanding and kindly toward him because his conscience must be giving him an awfully rough time.[174]

Devil Girl from Mars (Lion, 1955) was a British import which featured an extraterrestrial femme fatale and her troublesome robot;

---

[172]Ralph Gerstlé, "Film Reviews," Films in Review, January, 1955, pp. 34-35.

[173]Lloyd Shearer, "The Movies' New Craze—Horror," Parade, April 20, 1958, p. 12.

[174]Charles Beaumont, "The Science Screen," The Magazine of Fantasy and Science Fiction, December, 1955, p. 70.

and King Dinosaur (Lippert, 1955) marked the debut of young writer-director Bert I. Gordon, who shot the whole thing in a week at Big Bear, California for $15,000. It grossed over a million.[175]

> Against all advice, and my better judgment, I went to see King Dinosaur, . . . and am still somewhat alarmed at the fun I had. I recommend it for one excellent reason: It is not only the worst s.f. picture ever made, . . . but also without question the worst picture of any sort ever made, in all respects. A blessed veil of forgetfulness has spared me any specific memories, except an absolutely hilarious battle between a Gila monster and a baby alligator. The Gila monster is, of course, supposed to be the Dinosaur. What the baby alligator is supposed to be, I couldn't say.[176]

The Revenge of the Creature (Universal, 1955) saw the return of the Gill Man, who this time is captured and taken to an oceanarium, from which, of course, he promptly escapes.

> Nothing whatever can stop the gill-man, . . . for he is protected by the strongest force-field in existence: Money. The critics did their best to kill him off directly after his appearance in The Creature from the Black Lagoon, but he is going strong again in The Revenge of the Creature, and it is only too clear from the ending of this particular disaster that we have by no means seen the last of him. It's true that he is shot, but this doesn't fool anybody; after all, to a studio resourceful enough to explain how Frankenstein's monster managed to survive a bath of lava, what are a few lousy bullets?
>
> The Creature is after Lori Nelson in this one, incidentally—for what dark reasons only he knows. When he finally gets her, he has no idea what to do with her, except swim. This provides the

---

[175] Hollis Alpert and Charles Beaumont, "The Horror of It All," Playboy, March, 1959, p. 76.

[176] Charles Beaumont, "The Science Screen," The Magazine of Fantasy and Science Fiction, March, 1956, p. 73.

necessary pathos, as well as most of the action.[177]

Tarantula! (Universal, 1955) made no bones about providing a satisfactory monster—a spider as big as a house, created by mad scientist Leo G. Carroll, menaced the countryside until brought low by napalm bombs.

No sooner was this creature subdued, than another and bigger beast heaved itself out of the ocean to prey upon long-suffering humanity in It Came from Beneath the Sea (Columbia, 1955):

> It Came from Beneath the Sea is, I fear, the best of the new ones, due mainly to the excellent special effects work of Ray Harryhausen. George Worthington Yates and Hal Smith collaborated on the screenplay, and though it is seldom downright painful, it is both technically and dramatically anemic, and remains upright only with the help of a dozen or so sturdy clichés. Mr. Yates is a competent hand, but I'm sorry to report that this science fiction continues to baffle him. He is never strictly at home in this film except during the love sequences; these, however, are frequent enough to sustain his interest . . . while murdering ours.
>
> What comes from beneath the sea this time is an octopus, by the way. It's a perfectly ordinary octopus, except that it is radioactive, approximately the size of the Chrysler building, and hungry. One of many such giants residing in the Great Mindanoan Deep, it would have been content to stay at home with the wife and children forever, if only we humans had not begun to monkey around with hydrogen bombs. But one of our Marshall Island experiments explodes in the neighborhood and the beast is instantly rendered radioactive. Forced to give up its everyday cuisine, for now it warns off its natural prey, . . . it takes to attacking liners and eventually decides to feast upon San Francisco. Unfortunately, a little common sense could have stopped the monster—and the film too—after 15 minutes.[178]

---

[177]Beaumont, "The Science Screen," December, 1955, op. cit., pp. 69-70.

[178]Ibid., p. 69.

Even This Island, Earth (Universal, 1955), a lavish Technicolor production based on the novel by Raymond F. Jones, featured a rather hideous monster—a half-insect, half-human mutant from another planet. There was plenty in this film for the old-time science-fiction fan to have fun with: a strange machine called an "interociter," a sort of super TV set; a flying saucer; green life-saving rays that prevent a plane from crashing; death rays that blow up station wagons; high-domed extra-terrestials; flaming, guided meteors; an alien, surrealistic planet at war with another one, and many other marvels. The special effects were well done, for the most part, and the whole thing was rousing good fun.

> This Island, Earth stays earth-bound just a little too long as Scientist Rex Reason grows increasingly suspicious of a house party thrown by Jeff Morrow, an eggheaded visitor from outer space. But when Rex and his beautiful fellow scientist Faith Domergue try to escape, they are scooped into a flying saucer and whizzed off to the planet of Metaluna to help their hard-pressed host fight off some neighboring spacemen. The interplanetary war that follows has Metaluna looking like a giant pinball machine screaming "Tilt!" in seven different colors. What with dodging flaming meteors and grappling with odious mutants (half-human and half-insect monsters that have a weakness for female earthlings), Rex and Faith are might lucky to grab a seat on the last spaceship back to earth.[179]

El Super Sabio (The Super Scientist) (1955) was a somewhat more refined, if sillier, import from Mexico, starring Cantinflas; Britain contributed The Thirteenth Moon of Jupiter (1955);

---

[179]"Cinema," Time, July 11, 1955, p. 94.

Czechoslovakia made Journey to a Primeval Age (1955), directed by Karel Zeman, in color; Johnny Weissmuller starred in Jungle Moon Men (Columbia, 1955), and Come In, Jupiter (USC, 1955) was an experimental 16mm color short, made by students in the University of Southern California Cinema Department, "dealing with the international problems of race, peace and war. A 'Martian' reports on his findings after visiting earth."[180]

George Pal released his newest Technicolor science-fiction film in 1955, but unfortunately, The Conquest of Space (Paramount), for which everyone had had such high hopes, was something of a disappointment:

> Here is certainly the disappointment of the year, if not of all time; by all odds one of the worst science fiction movies ever made. With a fine book (by Willy Ley and Chesley Bonestell) as his nominal base, and with a stable of top-notch writers—James O'Hanlon, Barré Lyndon, George Worthington Yates, and Oscar-winner Philip Yordan—assigned to the screenplay, George Pal has done science fiction its greatest disservice since Abbott and Costello Go to Mars. At least that picture was honest. Conquest of Space is not. It is mendacious, pompous, packed to bursting with all the clichés that ever were or ever will be, and utterly tasteless. What plot there is, is negligible. The special effects are uniformly poor, however correct they may be from a technical standpoint. At no time is a scene built up or handled with even the minimal skill one would expect from a Katzman quickie—let alone from the men who made Destination Moon. Bang! We're on the space platform. Pow! We're on Mars! Boom! Off again. The

---

[180] "University of Southern California Film Catalogue" (Los Angeles: Department of Cinema, The University of Southern California, 1958), p. 22.

end.[181]

The year 1955 also saw the production of some fine science documentaries, which are mentioned here because they each contained some flights of speculation and fancy such as the fascinating tour around the solar system in the Russian-made *The Great Universe*, produced by the Leningrad Studio of Popular Films.

> *The Great Universe* (on both 16mm and 35mm) is to be highly recommended. The subject is well handled, there is good commentary, and the animated diagrams and models are very effective. The film is only medium length, of course, and its compass is therefore necessarily confined to reference to Soviet research.[182]

Walt Disney also produced his now-famous TV documentary of space flight, *Man in Space* in 1955, which featured Dr. Wernher Von Braun, Willy Ley, and Dr. Heinz Haber in a fascinating partly-animated discussion of space flight, its past and its future. The adventures of the little cartoon spaceman were humorous and instructive, and the final sequence was real science-fiction, a realistically animated trip into outer space in a three-stage rocket. This film was re-edited and released theatrically in Technicolor and wide screen, in 1957. Disney also produced a sequel for TV, *Man and the Moon*, the same year, which continued the kind of thing begun in *Man in Space*. It was not

---

[181] Charles Beaumont, "The Science Screen," *The Magazine of Fantasy and Science Fiction*, September, 1955, p. 49.

[182] Bernard Orna, "New Films," *Films and Filming*, May, 1955, p. 18.

theatrically released, but contained an excellent live-action trip around the moon.

And so, the so-called "Golden Years" of the science-fiction film drew to a close. The period 1950 through 1955 had seen a gratifying resurgence of science-fiction pictures, including some of the best ever made, but by the beginning of 1956, although there were still a few excellent ones to come, quality production had begun to drop off in favor of the more sensational "science-horror" films. The monsters got bigger and bigger, giant creatures of every description attacked this poor, beleaguered planet, and good, thought-provoking science-fiction became more and more scarce.

IV. THE DECLINING YEARS: 1956 AND 1957

Jules Verne once again found his wondrous works on the screen in 1956, with the magnificently spectacular version of *Around the World in 80 Days*, produced in Technicolor and Todd-AO by the late Michael Todd. This great, sprawling motion picture, a giant travelogue directed with warmth and humour by Michael Anderson, has been playing to capacity houses all over the world continuously ever since its release, and is known to virtually every man, woman and child in the civilized world. Starring David Niven as Phileas Fogg, the man who wagers a fortune that he can traverse the globe in 80 days—and wins—this film captured the spirit of adventure and wonder that Jules

Verne tried to put into his novels, and qualifies as science-fiction only on a technicality: the fact that at the time it was written, Fogg's feat had never been done. Like King Kong, too much has been written about Around the World in 80 Days to warrant further discussion here; but it is large enough to claim space in any film history.

The year 1956 produced quantity but little quality in the way of science-fiction. Such films as The Atomic Man (Allied Artists, 1956), The Beast of Hollow Mountain (United Artists, 1956), The Brain Machine (RKO, 1956), The Day the World Ended (ARC, 1956), Fire Maidens of Outer Space (Topaz, 1956), It Conquered the World (American-International, 1956), The Phantom from 10,000 Leagues (ARC, 1956) and The She-Creature (American-International, 1956) did nothing to enhance the reputation of science-fiction to any one but the teen-agers, who by this time formed the largest portion of the audiences. Out of the above potpourri, the earth was menaced by: a man whose mind worked in the future; a prehistoric "RegiScope" allosaurus; a three-eyed, horned mutant; death-dealing fire-women; a giant, fanged cucumber-like creature from Venus; a sea-serpent; and a lobster-lady, transformed into a clawed sea-beast by a hypnotist.

Bela Lugosi returned to pictures this year, after a long illness, and made a pitiful film called Bride of the Monster (Catacomb, 1956), which was so poorly made as to be embarrassing to watch. All the fire had gone out of Bela, and he was old and tired; his body and face were wasted from the effects of his long sickness, and it was no wonder that he passed away soon after completing his last film, Plan 9 from Outer Space, which has not as yet been released. In Bride of the Monster Bela played around with atomic rays, creating a giant octopus, to which he fed his victims.

And the Gill Man was back once again! In The Creature Walks Among Us (Universal, 1956) he is transformed surgically into an air-breathing being, after a fire burns off his gills, but he still has the same old nasty temper:

> The monster of The Creature Walks Among Us (third in a series) is the more revolting for being only slightly bigger than man-size, and very nearly a man. He is what a man would look like if a man were a catfish—something like an iguana without a tail. He is equipped with both gills and lungs. The scientists try to domesticate him, but things presently go sickeningly awry. . . . the Creature is a fish out of water to perfection.[183]

Another aquatic monstrosity, this one from Japan, was Godzilla (Toho, 1956), the first Japanese science-fiction film of any note and the first to gain a popular release in this country. It was produced by Tomoyuki Tanaka and directed by Terry Morse and Ishiro Honda. The Japanese, with perhaps more justification, also put the blame on the H-Bomb for disturbing their monster, a gigantic "whatsis" that rises out of the sea and lays waste to large areas of Tokyo.

> The Japanese, once famous in American economic folklore for their imitation Amazonian shrunken heads, Confederate flags, and

---

[183] "Movies," Newsweek, May 14, 1956, p. 126.

> American-looking gadgets, have now turned their attention to the King Kong type of movie. Godzilla features what looks like a 400-foot-high plucked chicken, which emerges from the Sea of Japan and, understandably, terrorizes Tokyo. The movie could very easily pass for an old American one. . . . Japan's enormous "Godzilla" and America's "Creature" both make exactly the same, bubbling croak when offended; otherwise, there is no comparison. Godzilla cannot act his way out of a paper bag . . .[184]

Nobody seemed to be sure just exactly what Godzilla really was:

> . . . Godzilla turns out to be a cross between a tyrannosaurus, a large dragon and our old friend King Kong. Estimated 400 feet tall, he roars like a lion, emits great quantities of fire from his ugly mouth, and occasionally waves his front paws in a pathetic, rather dazed manner. Emerging from Tokyo Bay, Godzilla lays waste large areas of the city before being destroyed in an underwater ambush by a Japanese scientist armed with an agent designed to destroy the oxygen in water. Extensive special effects and model work help to create an authentic impression of chaos, as Godzilla rampages over skyscrapers, bridges and streets; and his final disintegration, amid a wild confusion of bubbles and threshing limbs, is effectively managed.
>
> Judged simply as another excursion into a gruesome fantasy world, the film merits little more attention than its American or British predecessors. However, an underlying note of social protest is apparent in the characterisation (the scientist is at first reluctant to unleash his terrible secret even against the monster); also, Godzilla's radio-active appearance is directly attributed to H-bomb experiments. A more obvious symbolic sequence shows a long line of maimed bodies followed by a children's choir singing a prayer for deliverance. . . . So this fusion of fantasy and reality inevitably harks back to the events of eleven years ago.[185]

The Indestructible Man (Allied Artists, 1956) found Lon Chaney, Jr. back doing just about what he did in The Man-Made Monster (1941),

---

[184]Ibid.

[185]James Morgan, "Film Reviews: In Brief," Sight and Sound, Winter, 1956-57, p. 154.

re-released in 1953 as The Atomic Monster. Once again, he's all full of electricity and atomic power (to bring it up to date), and nothing can get rid of him save an overdose of what he thrives on—atomic power.

The Mole People (Universal, 1956) revealed a lost civilization of Sumerians and their slaves, living underground. The mole men were rather sickening to look upon, and a prologue by USC's Dr. Frank Baxter assured the audience that it was all quite possible . . .

Satellite in the Sky (Warner Bros., 1956) was a WarnerColored, CinemaScope, British-made story about the launching of an earth satellite and the testing of a tremendously powerful "tritonium bomb," which can only be exploded in space. It is far more powerful than a hydrogen bomb and to detonate it on earth would be disastrous.

> This latest edition to the space films I found rather dreary. . . . directed by ex-documentary man Paul Dickson. A note of authenticity is aimed at (the ship, we are told in a hand-out, "could really fly") but the plot, together with a shambling handling of themes soon gets rid of that.[186]

A group of scientists—including a stowaway girl reporter—take the bomb up in a rocket ship to test it in space, but it attaches itself to the ship instead of flying off into the void. It is timed to go off, and the crew of the ship find themselves in something of a predicament, for if they return to earth, the bomb will kill millions. This could have been an exciting and suspenseful picture, but "Jerky cutting, stagey effects,

---

[186]Ken Gay, "New Films," Films and Filming, October, 1956, p. 27.

ham acting and the triteness of the plot destroy the smooth horror and evocation of thought that a film on this subject might have created."[187]

Invasion of the Body Snatchers (Allied Artists, 1956) was a step in the right direction, it seemed. Here was some good, solid suspenseful science-fiction, with believable human characters and an ingenious, horrifying menace. Based on a Collier's serial by Jack Finney, it told of the gradual taking over of a small town in California by a malignant form of plant life which formed itself into exact duplicates of people living there, after disposing of their bodies.

World without End (Allied Artists, 1956) was another big Technicolor CinemaScope production starring Hugh Marlowe and Nancy Gates, which told of a group of space pilots who take off in a rocket and suddenly find themselves going faster than they ever intended. Their speed increases until it is beyond the realms of believability, and they black out. When they regain consciousness, they land the ship on what they believe to be another planet, but they eventually discover, after a series of encounters with deformed mutants and giant spiders, that they are still on earth—only 500 years into the future!

It seems they hit a "time warp," which threw them forward in time to the year 2508 A. D., when an atomic war has driven those not mutated underground, and they soon join forces with the inhabitants of

---

[187] Ibid.

an underground city to fight off the mutants. There is a short-skirted future girl for each of the crew members, of course, and eventually they drive away all the mutants with home-made bazookas and settle down to build "a better world."

The Gamma People (Columbia, 1956) was a strange hybrid of a film: on one hand, it was a delightful spoof of science-fiction films, complete with mad scientist and gleaming Flash Gordon death ray; and on the other, it was played quite seriously, for all the suspense and horror possible. Paul Douglas played his role broadly throughout, and there was an almost surrealistic quality to the film at times, particularly during the night scenes:

> Like a bad dream this film describes the adventures of two newspapermen who accidentally enter a small Graustarkian nation ruled by a mad scientist. The comic-opera aspects of the isolated country, with its gaily costumed police force and people, its quaint buildings, and its lack of communications, contrast strongly with the reality beneath the surface. The insane scientist, in an effort to develop geniuses, experiments with gamma rays upon children. His mistakes provide an army of "goons," which under his direction terrorize the inhabitants. . . . neither a credible, realistic horror story nor a fantasy.[188]

Earth vs. the Flying Saucers (Columbia, 1956) presented a good deal of interesting special effects by Ray Harryhausen, as a fleet of flying saucers do battle with the United States Army over Washington, D. C. Inhabited by what appear to be faceless robots with built-in

---

[188]"Motion Picture Previews," National Parent Teacher, June, 1956, p. 37.

death rays in each hand, the saucers shoot down satellites, kidnap earthlings, threaten women, crash into the Washington Monument and demolish the Capitol while Hugh Marlowe, Donald Curtis, Joan Taylor and others try to stop them.

U. F. O. (Unidentified Flying Objects) (United Artists, 1956) was an interesting semi-documentary on flying saucers, featuring interviews with people who actually "saw" them, and featuring some unremarkable-looking "actual footage" of U.F.O.'s. Two very good science-fiction films, produced in Britain by a newly-formed company, Hammer Films, crept almost unobserved into American cinemas among all the others. Because of its lurid title, the first one, The Creeping Unknown (United Artists, 1956) caught many critics unaware:

> For the benefit of those who, like myself, may have been put off by the advertising, I must report that the film was based on an original play The Quatermass Experiment, by that eminent short-story writer, Nigel Kneale. Quatermass (played superbly by Brian Donlevy) is a rock-hard, icy-veined scientist who has launched the first spaceship. As the movie begins, the ship is crashing back to Earth. Authorities investigate it and are presented with a dilemma worthy of John Dickson Carr. Whereas there had been three crew members inside the craft at takeoff, only one — Victor Carroun — can be found . . . and the air-lock was not opened! . . . The police become interested and we divide our time between investigating the problem of the two missing men and wondering what has happened to the remaining one. He is in a state of shock. But, Quatermass sees, there's more than that the matter with him. In fact, according to the medical tests, this chap ought to be dead! He is hospitalized for further study, which piques his wife. She arranges for a shady character to spirit Victor away from the dreadful place. Unfortunately, Victor is not entirely Victor; he is a Thing possessed—by what, we don't know. And the Thing, after frightening Mrs. Carroun into apoplexy and killing her confederate, goes on a rampage. Quatermass examines the murdered man and

> finds only an empty skin. He finds a shattered vase and some cactus needles in the hospital room. He begins to ponder the possibilities of alien life forms in space . . . and the fun really begins. . . . it is all enormously suspenseful. . . .
>
> The photography, the direction (particularly in the zoo sequence) and the acting (excepting his wife) are magnificently done, quite worthy of Lewton's best. And if the ending is a bit hurried and pat, one can easily reflect that perfection is always dull.[189]

But that ending is one of the most horrifying in all of science-fiction: for at last director Val Guest lets us see what Victor has become —the alien monstrosity in all its loathsomeness. This creature is a sickening, sentient-looking mass of sheer evil, truly one of the most masterful jobs of monster-making in the entire history of science-fiction and horror films

The sequel to this film, titled Quatermass II in England, was released in this country as Enemy from Space (United Artists, 1956). Brian Donlevy again starred, and Val Guest again directed. This one was good, but not up to the high standards of suspense and terror set by the original:

> This is a fair to middling piece of British Science Fiction, generous with its lupoid visual horrors, but short on imaginative ideas and atmosphere. The script, faithfully adapted from Nigel Kneale's television serial, covers similar ground to Invasion of the Body Snatchers. . . but is not quite up to the standard. . . .
>
> Intruders from some unknown asteroid descend on the lonely village of Winnerden Flats, and lie all over the countryside imprisoned in small rocket-shaped meteorites. These meteorites

---

[189] Charles Beaumont, "The Science Screen," The Magazine of Fantasy and Science Fiction, December, 1957, p. 64.

burst open in the face of anyone picking them up. The injured person immediately becomes victim to the "superior intelligences" hidden within each of these hollow, symmetric stones.

> All this would be more chilling if only the film did not give such an impression of having been rushed. Although made by the same technical unit . . . this Quatermass sequel misses the impressive scenes of location, of ordinariness to counterpoise the fantastic, which was conveyed by the earlier film. The dialogue is slack and the acting is variable, with only Sidney James and John Van Eyssen bringing the absolute conviction to their roles necessary in this kind of tall story.[190]

But by the very terms in which the reviewers were coming to speak of these films, one can see how they were coming to think more and more of the science-fiction and horror film as the same thing. As indeed, it was fast becoming. But two films stood out in 1956 as representatives of good, solid "pure" science-fiction. The first of these was another British-made film, Holiday Productions' adaptation of George Orwell's grimly prophetic novel, <u>1984</u> (Columbia, 1956). Directed by Michael Anderson of <u>Around the World in 80 Days</u> fame, the film starred Edmond O'Brien, Jan Sterling and Michael Redgrave.

> The surprisingly candid producer of this British-made film says it has been "freely adapted from Orwell's novel, and so it has. But not inappositely, nor ineffectually. A love affair between Edmond O'Brien and Jan Sterling, which preoccupies much of the footage, does not <u>seem</u> extraneous, for we need relief from the political rigors that are the film's prime concern. These rigors are like none the world has ever seen. And may it never see them.
>
> . . . .

---

[190]Peter John Dyer, "New Films," <u>Films and Filming</u>, May, 1957, p. 28.

> In a political tract such as <u>1984</u> characters are rarely if ever individualized. They weren't in Orwell's novel, and they aren't in this film. For this, the scriptwriters — William T. Templeton and Ralph Bettinson — are responsible. Do not blame the director, who, on the whole, did quite well.[191]

Purists were happy to discover that the film retained the grim, unhappy ending of the novel, as there were rumors during production of a happy "Hollywood ending." This was a difficult and courageous movie to make, and despite its lack of characterization, it was serious science-fiction for a change, in the tradition of <u>Things to Come</u> and <u>Metropolis</u>.

> Things to come, as George Orwell saw them in his clever anti-totalitarian tract, written in 1949, have assumed a horrifying political shape by 1984. The State is everything, terror is normalcy, love is a crime. Political shapes, however, are not the kind that lure millions to the movies, even in an election year.[192]

The plot deals with the revolt of one man, Winston Smith (Edmond O'Brien) and his sweetheart (Jan Sterling) against the society of 1984, where the Anti-Sex League tries day and night to eliminate love of any kind. They elude detection until they are befriended by Michael Redgrave, whom they think is a member of a secret fifth column against the government of "Big Brother." But Big Brother is everywhere, and Redgrave betrays them into the hands of the Thought Police, where, under physical and mental tortures, they are made to recant and accept the rule of the State. The sets are well done, adding much to the

---

[191] Henry Hart, "Film Reviews," <u>Films in Review</u>, November, 1956, pp. 463-464.

[192] "Cinema," Time, October 8, 1956, p. 108.

atmosphere and mood of the film, but the process backgrounds are sometimes too jiggly. The all-seeing TV eye, installed in every room in every building, is as forbidding as many a live monster. . . .

The second film to return to the "good old days" of science-fiction was a lavish, excellently-made CinemaScope science-fiction spectacle, Forbidden Planet (MGM, 1956). Produced by Nicholas Nayfack and directed by Fred Wilcox, this film was a terrific treat for science-fiction fans, with myriads of Technicolored delights for the eye, and wondrous electronic sounds for the ear.[193] It starred Anne Francis, Walter Pidgeon and Leslie Nielson, and introduced a fantastic robot with real character—"Robby."

> Taken at its intended level, M-G-M's Forbidden Planet (screenplay by Cyril Hume, on a story by Irving Block and Allen Adler, direction by Fred Wilcox) is surprisingly good. As with most of us, I had listened to the razzmatazz publicity for a year and built up a nice healthy resistance to the film, frankly expecting sort of a combination of Conquest of Space and Robot Monster. As it turns out, the picture is quite consistent with its aim—which is, simply, to entertain—and although there are many flaws (muddy plot development, outrageous padding, heavy dependence upon clichés, occasionally embarrassing dialogue) it would take a very sour reviewer indeed to deny that it is still spanking good fun. The story, except for one startlingly unique twist, is familiar stuff:

---

[193]Instead of an ordinary music score, the producer wanted something different for this film, something more in keeping with the nature of the picture. So the "music" was composed of "Electronic Tonalities," performed on electronic instruments by Bebe and Louis Barron. The result was wonderfully alien and eerie. See: Philip K. Scheuer, "A Town Called Hollywood: Wail of Tortured Electrons Provides Eerie Film Score," Los Angeles Times, February 26, 1956, part IV, p. 2.

Space Patrol goes to farflung star system to locate missing expedition; mysterious voice warns troops away, but to no avail. The Patrol lands and finds the strange and wonderful world of the extinct super-race, the Krell—a world of mind-staggering technological development. All of the members of the original expedition are dead with the exception of Doctor Morbius (played competently, if a shade resignedly, by Walter Pidgeon) and his daughter, Altaira (Anne Francis). What has happened? Morbius does not know, only that some Evil Force did the others in while leaving him and the girl untouched. Now he is busily engaged in trying to unlock the secrets of the Krell, and would like nothing better than to wave goodbye to the Patrol. The Commander of the ship, however, is reluctant to leave and refuses to do so until specific orders are received from Earth. Enter the Evil Force, in the form of an invisible monster . . . (The unique twist is that the monster is actually the rampageous Id of kindly Dr. Morbius himself, and only with his death can the creature be destroyed. To my way of thinking, a perfectly grand basis for a whole new picture.)

At this point we are offered divertissement. Miss Francis performs what may be described as a Morbius strip (she has never seen an Earthman other than her father and considers the Commander "perfectly lovely!" It gets gooey along about this time, and the possibilities are never really tapped. . . .

It must be stated at once that all of this is made wholly bearable by the special effects work, which is incredibly good. Walt Disney's studio was employed for this purpose, and the boys outdid themselves.[194] The only fair descriptive word would be stunning. In fact, I will go out on a limb and state that Bonestell himself could not have surpassed the genuinely beautiful yet always alien terrain of Altair; and as for the Krell workshops, with their countless gimmicks and gadgets, and the big tunnel which stretches miles below the surface of the planet—these are the finest examples of the art that I have seen to date. . . .

The picture fairly bursts at the seams with technical triumphs of this sort. The much touted Robby the robot looks silly at first glance, but pretty soon—despite its alarming resemblance to a

---

[194]For a detailed explanation of how many of the special effects were achieved, see: George Folsey, "The Filming of Forbidden Planet," American Cinematographer, August, 1955, pp. 460-461, 482-484.

> slot machine—you forget that it is just a thick rubber suit with a very uncomfortable man inside and find yourself charmed by the creation. Anything but charming is the Monster. The animators worked nine months to do the single short sequence wherein we get a look at the Id-beast, and I must say that it was no waste of time. The thing looks something like a gigantic, vaguely anthropomorphic lion, something like a fighting bull, . . . and it is guaranteed to scare the liver and lights out of you.
>
> . . . .
>
> Forbidden Planet's best moments evoke the innocent old-time wonders of science-fiction and are purely delightful; its worst can be forgiven. The kids—for whom, after all, it was made—will stampede to it, and I, for one, propose to join them. I suggest you do, too.[195]

Our final year, 1957, brought an unprecedented number of science-fiction films to the screens, some 32 in all, but the public was beginning to get too much. As the pictures became more ridiculous and more repetitious, the audiences began to laugh—and then stay away. More and more pure "horror" films were beginning to come out, replacing the "science-fictions," spurred by the revival on television of Universal's old Frankenstein and Dracula thrillers. New versions of Frankenstein and Dracula were burgeoning, and the science-fiction films tried to cash in on this trend by substituting shock value for story and characterization. Only a very few stand out during the concluding year of this study.

The Abominable Snowman of the Himalayas (Regal, 1957) was

---

[195] Charles Beaumont, "The Science Screen," The Magazine of Fantasy and Science Fiction, June, 1956, pp. 79-81.

another of the Hammer Films productions, a better-than-average treatment of the "Abominable Snowman" theme, directed by Val Guest. Forrest Tucker and Peter Cushing starred in this "imaginatively produced"[196] film, which described a search for the snowmen, or "Yeti," and the subsequent discovery of them by a party of five men. They turn out to be "a race of super-intelligent beings who figure on taking over the world when humanity has destroyed itself."[197]

But for every intelligently-written-and-directed science-fiction film, there seemed to be three or four of the increasingly monotonous "giant creature" pictures:

The Amazing Colossal Man (American-International, 1957) was the brainchild of producer-writer-director Bert I. Gordon. A former Army colonel who is horribly burned in an accidental plutonium explosion starts to grow at the rate of 10 feet a day. "He destroys part of Los Vegas and carries off his own fiancée before he is brought down by bullets."[198]

Attack of the Crab Monsters (Allied Artists, 1957) featured huge atomically-mutated crabs who menace a party on a remote Pacific island; Beginning of the End (Republic, 1957) had the world menaced by a plague of giant grasshoppers, realistically portrayed by live insects,

---

[196]"Motion Picture Reviews," Daily Variety, October 28, 1957, p. 3.

[197]Ibid. [198]Shearer, op. cit., p. 14.

not models. The Black Scorpion (Warner Bros., 1957) was the baby of old-timer Willis O'Brien, in which giant scorpions crawl out of a lost underground cavern and terrorize Mexico. The Cyclops (Allied Artists, 1957) was another plain human menace, but enlarged to gigantic proportions by "high radiation" in a lost Mexican canyon, along with other animals there. His face was horribly disfigured in the plane crash that brought him there, and he had only one eye left; hence his name. The Deadly Mantis (Universal, 1957) was another "script-written-around-a-monster" idea of producer William Alland, the only insect he could think of at the time that hadn't been used.[199] The Giant Claw (Columbia, 1957) was probably the silliest beast of the lot, a huge roc-like bird from outer space, composed of "anti-matter," which doesn't register on radar screens. Produced by Sam Katzman, this interstellar fowl looked like something Al Capp might draw. Half-Human (DCA, 1957) was another abominable snowman story, this one made in Japan and starring John Carradine. Invasion of the Saucer Men (American-International, 1957) was a teen-age comedy thriller, featuring midget Martians with huge, cabbage-like heads and detachable hands (each with its own eye) which went around injecting people with alcohol, making them drunk or killing them; Godzilla Raids Again (Toho, 1957) showed that the Japanese knew a good thing when they saw

---

[199] Alpert and Beaumont, *op. cit.*, p. 88.

it—the giant beast, apparently heedless of his demise in the first film, in true Frankenstein-Gill Man tradition, was up to his old tricks again until stopped by another, equally ferocious monster called Anzilla. This was a clear case of fighting fire with fire.

Kronos (Regal, 1957) featured an interesting idea, produced and directed by the late Kurt Neumann: a giant metal cube, a power-hungry space ship from another world, lands on earth and soaks up all the electrical and atomic energy it can find until finally overloaded and blown to atoms. *The Land Unknown* (Universal, 1957) was an unremarkable journey to a lost prehistoric continent, hardly a novel idea by this time. The dinosaurs merely looked ludicrous, even in CinemaScope. *Monster From Green Hell* (DCA, 1957) had giant wasps buzzing around the African jungle; *The Monster that Challenged the World* (United Artists, 1957) was a huge, incredibly fecund sea-caterpillar, or shell-less snail; *Not of This Earth* (Allied Artists, 1957) featured "vampires from outer space."

Rodan (Toho, 1957) was another Japanese production, this one in color, concerning a gigantic prehistoric bird, something like a giant pterodactyl, revived by atom blasts (of course). This newest pet of the King Brothers roared through the air at supersonic speeds, disintegrating jet planes, and the air blast from its wings laid waste to half of Tokyo—again!

And to top off this gruesome bunch of world-menacers, *20*

Million Miles to Earth (Columbia, 1957) offered an import from Venus, a scaly creature called an "Ymir," built along the lines of a tyrannosaurus, with a long, prehensile tail, sturdy, taloned hands and feet, an almost man-like torso, and a head that looked half-dragon, half-ape. It was quite fearsome, and novel, in that when it first arrived it was scarcely a foot high. But it grew rapidly, and after numerous mischiefs, including a fight with an elephant, it was tracked to the Coliseum in Rome and blasted to death by heavy artillery, having attained a height of around 50 or 60 feet. The monster was excellently animated, by Ray Harryhausen, and many of his movements put one in mind of old King Kong, who started all this back in 1933.

X the Unknown (Warner Bros., 1957) was another well-made Hammer production, starring Dean Jagger. This film was directed by Leslie Norman, but kept to the high standards of The Creeping Unknown in suspense, characterization and special effects. A change from interplanetary yarns or giant insects and crustaceans, the monster in X the Unknown was a roiling, radioactive lava-like substance that oozed up out of the ground and menaced the countryside:

> More localised than most blood-curdlers of visitations from outer space, action is confined to a desolate Scottish moor, where a platoon of soldiers is trained in using the Geiger counter to detect radioactivity. A large fissure in the ground appears; two men sustain radiation burns, one fatally. Others are similarly affected, one or two at the research station itself. The mysterious invasion is revealed as a mass of lava-like substance, finally

exorcised by a professor's counter-measures.[200]

The 27th Day (Columbia, 1957) was an excellent little film, another one of those "sleepers" that occur all too infrequently in the science-fiction field. Based on the novel by John Mantley, it was directed by William Asher and starred Gene Barry and Valerie French. There's not a monster in the whole picture, yet the suspense is gripping, except for a few scenes of overlong dialogue. An extraterrestrial visitor kidnaps five people from five different countries of the earth: a Chinese girl, a Russian soldier, a Los Angeles reporter, a British girl, and a German Professor. To each one he gives a small gold capsule—a bomb with enough power to detroy a continent. Each capsule can be opened and detonated only by its owner, and at the end of 27 days they will all become harmless. The film deals with the fate of these five people and their capsules; the frantic race by the governments of the world to find and destroy them before they can be used against one another. Finally, all are accounted for and destroyed except two—the one given to the Russian soldier and the one the American reporter has. Finally, through some clever thinking by the Professor and the discovery that the capsules have the power of both life and death, the world is saved and made peaceful as the Russian leaders are destroyed just as they were about to destroy the United

---

[200]P. L. Mannock, "New Films," Films and Filming, November, 1956, p. 24.

States.

The Incredible Shrinking Man (Universal, 1957) had been long awaited by fans of Richard Matheson, science-fiction author of The Shrinking Man, and it proved to be no disappointment. Indeed, in the excellence of its conception, it stood out as the best science-fiction picture of the year. The idea of a human being reduced in size had been used before, as in Paramount's Dr. Cyclops (1940), but this was a new approach to it. Based on Matheson's chilling novel, the film was a wonderful tour de force of all kinds of special effects:

> . . . The Incredible Shrinking Man relies on the art and ingenuity of its props, which were built on a gigantic scale so that a normal-sized actor would look small against them. This trick has been used in movies before, but never so dramatically. Everyday objects like scissors, pencils, mousetraps, a ball of twine and even a crumb of cake take on tremendous importance as they become magnified to the dwindling hero. He gets lost in his own cellar, fights a hungry spider and finally grows small enough to slip through a wire window screen.
>
> By hewing straight to the dilemma of the vanishing man, who battles to save his spirit as well as his life, Universal for a modest $700,000 has produced an outstanding science-fiction film which already has grossed $4 million.[201]

Producer Albert Zugsmith wisely commissioned Richard Matheson to do the screenplay from his own novel, so we have a faithful interpretation of the exciting and hair-raising book, uncluttered by any extraneous detail.

This movie's hero, . . . has a pretty good head on his shoulders,

---

[201] "Huge Props to Shrink a Man," Life, May 13, 1957, p. 143.

psychologically speaking; but disconcertingly his head, shoulders, and all the rest take to growing smaller. Eventually he is wriggling through the center of a window screen with no trouble at all.

One day while the normal-size hero, Scott Carey—played patiently by Grant Williams—is boating with his luscious blond wife they hit a fog bank which later proves to have been radioactive. This exposure plus contact with an insecticide has given Carey something called "an anti-cancer"—the opposite of excessive growth.

At any rate, one day he finds that his shirts and pants are getting too roomy. Shortly the sleeves of his bathrobe are clear down over his fingers. He starts to worry, and takes periodic measurements. Sure enough. Six months later we find him about the size of a stunted 5-year-old, but understandably, with grown-up satchels under his eyes. Despite his wife's sympathy, he begins to feel all alone in the world.

Soon Carey is living in a little doll house provided for him in the living room of his own home. He is now down to a height of slightly less than 4 inches. One day when his wife goes out the family tabby goes after its mouse-size master, who manages to escape (after the cat has toyed briefly with him). The unfortunate Lilliputian falls into the cellar and can neither get back upstairs nor make himself heard. He is presumed dead—of consumption by the cat—and the rest of this ingenious movie follows his solitary adventures in the cellar, foraging for food and defending himself from a height of 2 inches.

What makes the movie exceptional is the almost perfect illusion it manages to maintain of the hero actually existing, at whatever height he has shrunk to at any given moment, in the same world with his normal-size fellows. It is an illusion that took a powerful lot of creating, but the Universal studio people know that it was worth the trouble. Universal's "trick" pictures—the Frankenstein series, the invisible-man series, and others—have almost always been big box-office successes.[202]

This overwhelming illusion of reality shows how important good trick work is in maintaining credibility in science-fiction films. No monster

---

[202]"Movies," Newsweek, March 11, 1957, p. 106.

is more terrifying than that huge cat, reaching in through the windows of Scott Carey's doll house, because it is the familiar grown grotesque. The film offers no solution to the predicament, except "his own metaphysical comment: 'To God there is no zero. I *still* exist.' "[203] This is a strange ending, neither happy nor yet completely unhappy. It is rather metaphysically murky, but it is the ending of the novel.

The Invisible Boy (MGM, 1957) was an attempt to revive the popularity of Robby the Robot, star of *Forbidden Planet* the year before, but this film was vastly inferior to his first movie. There were some interesting effects, especially in portraying the giant calculator which begins to control the minds of young Richard Eyer and Robby himself (who temporarily becomes a heavy in this film), but the story was weak and the acting poor. The calculator, under the command of an evil force from outer space, is being used to conquer the world with rockets and missiles, and increases the brain potential of young Richard Eyer, whose father built the calculator. The boy puts together Robby, an old robot in his father's workshop, and Robby gives him the power of invisibility. Eventually, they smash the conspiracy together, and the world is saved. This film was the initial independent production of *Forbidden Planet*'s producer, Nicholas Nayfack, and it was not too successful.

---

[203] "Huge Props to Shrink a Man," *loc. cit.*

The Man Who Turned to Stone (Columbia, 1957) was a Katzman tale of a group of immortals whose flesh has been turned to living stone by absorbing the life-energies of countless hapless maidens whom they have destroyed over the centuries. Victor Jory and his crew of centuries-old fiends are ultimately detected by a psychiatrist turned private eye.

Speaking of being turned to stone, The Monolith Monsters (Universal, 1957) did just that to any and all living things that came in contact with them. This was a new kind of menace from outer space, made even more terrifying by its impersonality:

> . . . a mysterious meteorite . . . falls near a remote California community. When it comes in contact with water, the meteorite swells to huge proportions, and turns humans to stone in the process.
>
> Scientists Grant Williams [apparently restored to his normal height] and Trevor Bardette uncover this after several deaths. By this time, it's started to rain and the community, not to mention the entire country eventually, are threatened with total destruction. However, by frantic experimentation and a lucky guess, Williams comes up with the answer, the marching rocks can be stopped by common salt.[204]

The Night the World Exploded (Columbia, 1957) pitted the heroes of science against the very forces of nature itself, gone awry by the depletion of earth's natural oils and minerals. This is causing gigantic earthquakes which must be stopped or the world will be destroyed. Fortunately, "our science-fiction hero and his pretty

---

[204] "Film Reviews," Daily Variety, October 22, 1957, p. 3.

assistant [Kathy Grant] are equal to the task."[205]

In Outer Space Daze (Columbia, 1957) even the Three Stooges got into the science-fiction act, and Platillos Voladores (Flying Saucers) (1957) was a Mexican melodrama. Graduate students at the University of Southern California filmed an amusing 16mm short in color and VistaScope, Space Pirates, based on a short story, "The Nursery Commandos," by Adam Chase. A group of kids playing space pirate frighten off a real invasion of earth with their ray guns. The saucer men think the inhabitants too warlike to fight.

She-Devil (Regal, 1957) was another Kurt Neumann production, a fairly good picture about a scientifically created "Jekyll-and-Hyde" girl (Mari Blanchard).

> A consumptive waif is restored to health by a strange serum that destroys her feeling for humanity. Since she can change her appearance like a chameleon, her lovesick benefactor has difficulty in catching her when he decides to call a halt to her amoral activities, including murder.[206]

The following year, 1958, showed a continuation of the trend established by the preceding years, with more and more horror films being produced, and less and less good science fiction. Among such titles as Attack of the 50-Foot Woman, The Brain from Planet Arous, The Astounding She-Monster, The Spider, The Flame Barrier, Fiend

---

205 "Motion Picture Previews," National Parent Teacher, May, 1957, p. 37.

206 Ibid.

without a Face, Giant from the Unknown, It, The Terror from Beyond Space, The Hideous Sun Demon, The Lost Missile, The Blob, I Married a Monster from Outer Space, Terror from the Year 5,000, Missile to the Moon, Night of the Blood Beast, Queen of Outer Space, First Man into Space, War of the Colossal Beast, She-Demons, The Space Children, Teenage Caveman, War of the Satellites, Space Master X-7, The Cosmic Man, Monster on the Campus, The H-Man, The Mysterious Satellite, and Attack of the Puppet People, only a very few stood out: The Fly, From the Earth to the Moon, R. U. R., War with the Newts, Frankenstein 1970, and The Colossus of New York.

The future, however, does not look entirely black. There is still room for intelligent science-fiction pictures, if they are well-made and credible, with good, solid stories. Amid the general fall-off of science-fiction production in 1959, a few extremely interesting, big-budget films are in the works: George Pal is at last going to film H. G. Wells' classic, The Time Machine; Joseph M. Schenck is readying Jules Verne's A Journey to the Center of the Earth; and two end-of-the-world pictures are in preparation: Stanley Kramer's production of Nevil Shute's On the Beach, starring Tony Perkins, Fred Astaire, Gregory Peck, and Ava Gardner, and Sol C. Siegel's The World, the Flesh and the Devil, starring Harry Belafonte, Inger Stevens and Mel Ferrer.

Today's constant spotlight on fantastic advances in science will not let science-fiction rest. If productions of the calibre of those mentioned above can still be made, despite the decline in production of science-fiction generally, then perhaps there is hope for the science-fiction moviegoer. The future of this kind of film rests in the hands of men like George Pal and Walt Disney; perhaps they can instigate a new renaissance of good, healthy adult films, such as we saw in 1950, '51 and '52. We who recognize in the motion picture the ideal medium for the portrayal of science-fiction—just as Georges Méliès did, over half a century ago—devoutly hope so.

CHAPTER IV

AN EXAMINATION AND CRITICISM OF THE MERITS AND THE FAILINGS OF THE SCIENCE-FICTION FILM

I. ITS OBJECTIVES AND MEANS OF ACHIEVING THEM

As we glance back over the history of the science-fiction motion picture we will come to realize that the primary purpose of this type of film is to entertain. With few exceptions, writers, producers, cameramen, directors and actors have been attracted to science-fiction because they saw in it a chance to let their imaginations run rampant and provide new and different images, unbounded by conventionalities, for the delight of audiences. Ever since man first observed the starry heavens above him, he has been fascinated by the unknown, the worlds beyond ours, the possibilities of those two magic words, "what if . . . ?"

Secondarily, of course, science-fiction offers tremendous opportunities and possibilities for satire and moral reform. The film-maker's message, whatever it may be—from a gentle lampoon of current interests in technology and invention to a powerful protest against the horrors of nuclear warfare—can be vividly and imaginatively portrayed through the medium of science-fiction. As we have seen, writers of all ages have known this; Georges Méliès discovered it in his little laboratory in France.

Occasionally, we will find a film in which the "message" seemed to be its dominant raison d'être, as in They Came to a City or 1984, but whenever this occurs, the film inevitably suffers as a film. The story value is neglected and the characters become mere ciphers. By far the largest portion of science-fiction films have been and will continue to be theatrical in nature. They must entertain, they must recoup their costs, or they are not considered successful. Things to Come came dangerously close to overmoralizing, as did The Day the Earth Stood Still, but both were saved by the wealth of production value in them, the eye-filling spectacle and the interesting characters. Ralph Richardson's warlike "Boss"; Michael Rennie's Christ-like Klaatu; Rudolph Kleine-Rogge's maniacal Rotwang, in Metropolis; James Mason's fanatic Captain Nemo, and even the mechanical personality of Robby the Robot in Forbidden Planet. These are characters that stand out vividly in the memory, and cause one to recall the films in which they appeared. We will recall King Kong for years after all the giant insects and Godzillas are forgotten—not because he was the first of the giants, but because he had a unique personality. Thus, the films which can be considered classics in the field of science-fiction: Metropolis, Things to Come, The Lost World, The Day the Earth

Stood Still, The Thing, 20,000 Leagues Under the Sea (Disney) and the rest, have been those in which the entertainment values were put first and foremost, and the message came second. This does not mean that nothing is of value in a science-fiction film unless it entertains or amuses; one of the primary functions of science-fiction in any medium is to make men think. To open the imagination, to extrapolate the unknown, based on the known—this is the joy of science-fiction, the one form of literature where realism and fantasy blend to make the incredible believable.

Science-fiction offers escape, farther and faster than any other type of film; and this is one of the primary reasons why people go to the movies. They want to get far away from their often unappetizing existences, if only for a little while. They want to be able to say, after watching this or that future world, excitingly depicted, or some giant "thing" destroying a city, "I wish I could live in a world like that," or "I'm glad that was only a movie!" These are perhaps naïve thoughts, more often than not subconscious—but they are there. Good science-fiction cinema gives this to the viewer, gives him things to astound his senses, to make him think, perhaps, and conjecture on the possibilities of "what if . . . ?"

Basically, the factors which contribute toward making any science-fiction film an entertaining and enlightening piece of work are the same as those in any motion picture: good direction, editing, acting, camerawork, sound, special effects and—first and foremost—a good story to start from. Without these factors, whatever the science-fiction film is attempting to accomplish, be it pure entertainment, as in Forbidden Planet, or a serious treatment of class war, as in Aelita, cannot be successfully achieved. In this particular type of film, some of these elements of production take on special importance to the finished product; more so than in, say, a gangster movie or a comedy. The elements of camera and sound are two of the most important: for it is up to the camera to make the improbable visually credible, and the sound, by the introduction of new and novel sounds, as in The War of the Worlds, can stimulate the imagination greatly. The whole area of special effects work, optical and mechanical, assumes a major role in any good science-fiction film, above and beyond its utilization in other types of film. Well-done special effects, as in most of George Pal's films, can go a long way towards making the film believable; badly done, they cause only derision and laughter.

II. ITS SHORTCOMINGS AND POSSIBLE REMEDIES

The vast majority of science-fiction films which have been produced within the last few years have been low-budget, "quickie" films, hastily made to cash in on the popularity of the trend which began in 1950. Important production elements, such as story, acting and direction were neglected in favor of the "monster," or whatever the given menace happened to be. No longer did the science-fiction film attempt to astound and stimulate; its emphasis shifted to "shock value." Whatever devices that could be utilized in science-fiction to horrify, shock and even disgust, were crammed into the films, while more important elements went begging. We have seen the first few years' output (1950-1955) gradually turn from intelligent, well-thought-out films like Destination Moon, The Day the Earth Stood Still and War of the Worlds into a rash of "creature" pictures, almost identical in plot, and lacking, on the whole, even the rudiments of competent acting or direction. As in the case of The Creature from the Black Lagoon, scripts were often hastily thrown together around the given monster. "Think of a monster," the producers would say, "and we'll write a script around it." Charles Beaumont and Hollis Alpert discussed this:

> A more adaptable type was Martin Berkeley. He had established a reputation as a real pro, having written most of the Doctor Kildare and Lassie pictures, and therefore seemed the ideal choice for a series of horror films. Immediately upon signing the contract, he and Alland began the inevitable series of conferences. What sort of horror film should they make? They tried to think of stories, but that, selbstverständlich, got them nowhere. So, feeling that the gimmick was the thing foremost, they trotted down to the Los Angeles County Museum, where they looked at insects and other creatures in amber. Spiders had been used (Tarantula), so had ants (Them), so had lizards (King Dinosaur); but what about —the praying mantis? That was it! Berkeley returned to the studio and, after typing out a "formula sheet," based on the successful Them, reworked the picture as The Deadly Mantis. It made a million.[1]

---

[1]Alpert, Hollis, and Charles Beaumont, "The Horror of It All," Playboy, March, 1959, p. 88.

As a further example of where this type of thinking has led the science-fiction film, which by now has become equated with the horror film in most moviegoers' and critics' minds, consider that in one year (1957) the world was menaced by: a giant army officer, hideously burned; giant crabs; huge grasshoppers; giant scorpions; another human being, grown to huge and distorted proportions, and with only one eye; a giant praying mantis; a huge "bird" from outer space, composed of negative matter; Godzilla, a 400-foot-high Japanese monster; three different kinds of abominable snowmen; Martians with huge, bulbous heads and detachable hands; a huge calculator gone berserk and a robot; a giant metal cube; prehistoric dinosaurs; immortal men of living stone; giant crystals of rock; monstrous wasps; a giant amphibious caterpillar; subterranean earthquakes; vampires from outer space; an enormous prehistoric flying reptile; a rapidly-growing, dragon-like thing from Venus; a bubbling, radioactive ooze from under the earth and an all-devouring, subterranean fungus. Quite a roster of perils for one year.

The main ingredient which seems to be lacking in the conception of science-fiction films such as these, is story—something good and solid on which to base a shooting script. The science-fiction films of any given year which have been above the average, which have received the best critical acclaim, have been those based on established story material.

A glance at the most outstanding films in the *genre* down through the years will confirm this. Méliès, even, had his greatest success with *A Trip to the Moon*, based on Jules Verne's novel, *From the Earth to the Moon*; the Williamson Brothers' version of Verne's novel, *20,000 Leagues Under the Sea* (1916) was a success in its day; *Aelita*, the 1920 Russian film, was based on a play by Count Alexei Tolstoy; *Metropolis* was based on a novel by Thea von Harbou; *The Lost World* was the novel by Sir Arthur Conan Doyle; *The Invisible Man*, *Things to Come*, and *The Man Who Could Work Miracles* were all based on works by H. G. Wells; *King Kong* was based on a story by Edgar Wallace; *Destination Moon* was made from Robert A. Heinlein's *Rocket Ship Galileo*; *The Day the Earth Stood Still* was taken from a short story, "Farewell to the Master," by Harry Bates; *The Thing* came from a novelette by John W. Campbell, Jr., entitled "Who Goes There?"; *When Worlds Collide* was a dramatization of the Edwin Balmer-Philip Wylie novel; *War of the Worlds* was based on the H. G. Wells classic; *Around the World in 80 Days* was the Verne novel, as was Disney's *20,000 Leagues Under the Sea*; *The Incredible Shrinking Man* was based on the novel by Richard Matheson, and *The Fly*, a successful money-maker in 1958, was based on a short story in *Playboy* by George Langelaan.

Incidentally, almost all of these films have been big money-makers in their times, so there is no excuse for producers to scoff at good story material on that basis. The plain truth is that today too many of them are unwilling to pay for a good story, preferring to write one themselves, along a "formula line," or hire a relatively inexpensive writer to do one for them. They think a story is not necessary, as long as they've got a good gimmick. Unfortunately, this thinking has paid off financially for most of these producers to the disgust of critics, science-fiction fans, and many moviegoers in general, who no longer have any respect for the term "science-fiction" when applied to cinema. It has become synonomous with "horror." Monster-movie producer Bert Gordon said:

> In the first place, you've got to understand that the movie audience today consists almost entirely of teenagers. Either they're naïve and go to get scared, or they're sophisticated and enjoy scoffing at the pictures. There isn't much a teenager can scoff at these days, you know.[2]

Derek Hill, in a recent article in Sight and Sound, summed up the situation:

> The beginning of the new boom can be found in the science-fiction film of the early 'fifties. At first most of these concerned outward-bound rocket passengers, and any horror ingredients were disclosed en route or on arrival. Soon, though, the direction switched. The earth became subjected to attacks and visitations from outer space or beneath the sea (War of the Worlds, The Thing, The Beast from 20,000 Fathoms, Them!, etc.). Economically, this was a wise move. It is obviously cheaper to build one monster than a series of planet landscapes and props. Many of the visitors proved unintentionally comic rather than grim. Audiences laughed, but kept going back for more.

---

[2]Quoted in Ibid., p. 86.

It is impossible to pin-point exactly the beginning of the change. But as the monsters lost their initial novelty, the need for new sensationalism became recognised. Instead of using more imagination and invention in the presentation of the invaders, studios endeavoured to make each monster slimier and more repellent than its predecessor. The power of suggestion, the greatest tool of the vintage horror film, was abandoned. Instead, the screen began to concentrate on revolting close-ups. The obligatory last-reel death of the monsters provided plenty of opportunities. It was discovered, too, that details of damage done to human victims could be shown without disturbing the censor.

Soon almost every science fiction production included a few deliberately nauseating details of physical mutilation, which a few years ago the director would more effectively have suggested beyond the frame's borders. And this became as true of British as of American productions. Even the competent and not unimaginative _Quatermass_ films had their quota of closely observed melting heads and diseased flesh.[3]

Even serious studies of the science-fiction film, such as the above, tend to equate "science-fiction" with "horror." Thus far have such productions as those mentioned previously in this study brought us.

There is no doubt that these films "entertain" and "offer escape"—but to whom? The teenager and the moronic adult. It is not within the scope of this thesis to investigate the possible harmful effects of these cheaply-made "science-horror" films on children who watch them, but more and more, this problem is being discussed with growing alarm, as the films, now mostly supernatural or psychological horror films, continue to invade the screen.

Where, then, are the serious sociological studies like _Things to_

---

[3]Derek Hill, "The Face of Horror," _Sight and Sound_, Winter, 1958-59, p. 8.

Come and the original concepts of suspense like The War of the Worlds? One factor today is budget. The large sets and complicated effects called for in such films as Metropolis and Forbidden Planet are simply too expensive. But there are many good science-fiction stories which would make excellent, provocative screen entertainment if the producers of Hollywood would only search them out. Every science-fiction fan has his own list of favorite novels and stories that he would like to see put on the screen. Michel Laclos, in his book, Le Fantastique au Cinéma, mentions such possible works as City, by Clifford D. Simak; What Mad Universe, by Fredric Brown, and Richard Matheson's I Am Legend.[4] To these, this writer ventures to add a few more: Slan, by A. E. Van Vogt; In the Days of the Comet and Food of the Gods by H. G. Wells; Odd John and Sirius, by Olaf Stapledon; The Color Out of Space by H. P. Lovecraft; The Martian Chronicles and Fahrenheit 451 by Ray Bradbury; Robur the Conqueror by Jules Verne; One by David Karp; When the Sleeper Wakes by H. G. Wells; and The Scarlet Plague and The Iron Heel, by Jack London. By the use of these and other similar properties, Hollywood—and indeed, other countries—could once again bring the term "science-fiction" to the position of respect it once had in the film world. New classics could take their places beside the old. Some foreign producers have realized this, in

---

[4]Michel Laclos, Le Fantastique au Cinéma (Paris: Jean-Jacques Pauvert, 1958), p. xxxiv.

the recent production of such works as Karel Capek's R. U. R. (Italy, 1958) and the Czech production of Jules Verne's story "Face au Drapeau," An Invention of Destruction, voted "Best Film of 1958" at the World Film Festival at Brussels last summer.

In these days of incredibly rapid scientific advances, science-fiction has an obligation to focus men's minds on the positive as well as the negative aspects of science. Violence and shock values for their own sakes have no place in serious science-fiction; the challenge to the movie-maker is to present the world of the future or other worlds than ours imaginatively, originally, provocatively and entertainingly. Science-fiction can mean so much more than mere "monsters," as many films in the past have proved. Let the imaginations of creative producers, actors, writers, directors and technicians rove beyond the stale and the unimaginative; let their films precede man—outward to the stars!

CHAPTER V

SUMMARY AND CONCLUSIONS

Science-fiction as a form of literature dates back to the writings of Lucian of Samosata in the Second Century A. D. It has always been popular, but has run in cycles, such as the late 1800's and early 1900's, when the imaginative novels of Verne and H. G. Wells were great favorites.

The science-fiction film has a history of almost sixty years behind it, beginning with the filmic experiments in France of George Méliès. Méliès soon turned to the works of Jules Verne to provide fascinating stories for his imaginative and novel films. A Trip to the Moon and 20,000 Leagues Under the Sea, along with several science-fiction films, were very successful. Throughout the early years of the silent film, a number of interesting films were produced, dealing with science-fiction in one form or another, such as The Flying Torpedo, The Man from Mars, The Lost World, Metropolis, and The Girl in the Moon.

With the advent of sound in motion pictures, new dimension was given to science-fiction, and films such as High Treason, Berkeley Square, Just Imagine, The Invisible Man, and King Kong provided a tremendous escape mechanism for those beset by the miseries of the

Depression and the coming war in Europe. Science-fiction boomed in publishing, the comics, radio and in films, as serials like Flash Gordon and Buck Rogers began to be produced. However, a rash of horror films had begun with Frankenstein and Dracula in 1931, and science-fiction soon began to give way to horror. In 1936, H. G. Wells' Things to Come predicted the next war in 1940, but no one listened, and in 1938, Orson Welles made the world science-fiction conscious again with his famous scare-broadcast on radio of Wells' War of the Worlds.

The 'forties brought very little in the way of worthwhile science-fiction films, mostly cheap serials and horror films with only a few science-fiction gimmicks in them. Only a few films stand out in that period, such as J. B. Priestley's They Came to a City and Curt Siodmak's The Lady and the Monster.

But the 'fifties opened up a new renaissance in the science-fiction film. The end of the war and the marvels of the atom suggested new possibilities for science-fiction in film. George Pal started off the rush with his accurately-made Destination Moon, and soon the screen was crowded with films like The Thing, The Day the Earth Stood Still, The Man from Planet X, When Worlds Collide, and many more. This boom in "good" films continued until around 1955, when the smaller, more cheaply-made thrillers began to outnumber the bigger productions. As more and more of these small films were produced, they became preoccupied with horror and shock aspects to the exclusion of more important elements. Giant monsters and creatures of every sort menaced the earth again and again, in one formula-plot after another. By 1957, only a few worthwhile science-fiction films were produced, amidst a myriad of "cheapies." The year 1959 has seen a sharp decline in the popularity of these pictures, as even the teenage public, for whom they were consciously made, seems to have had enough. Gangster and western films are supplanting the "horror" cycle. But there is still hope for the future of science-fiction. Now that there will not be so many poorly-made films in circulation, bigger, more responsible producers can turn their talents toward science-fiction films based on good stories. Some are doing so now. If they are successful, more will follow. But the standards that govern any good work of film must be kept uppermost in these productions, if we are to see a return to the screen of true science-fiction, offering unlimited horizons of speculation, entertainment and escape.

BIBLIOGRAPHY

BIBLIOGRAPHY

A BOOKS

Agate, James. Around Cinemas. Amsterdam: Home and Van Thal, Limited, 1946. 280 pp.

Arnheim, Rudolf. Film as Art. Berkeley and Los Angeles: University of California Press, 1957. 230 pp.

Bailey, J. O. Pilgrims through Space and Time: Trends and Patterns in Scientific and Utopian Fiction. New York: Argus, 1947. 341 pp.

Benoit-Levy, Jean. The Art of the Motion Picture. Translated by Theodore R. Seackel. New York: Coward-McCann, 1946. 236 pp.

Cohn, Art (ed.). Michael Todd's Around the World in 80 Days Almanac. New York: Random House, 1956. 71 pp.

Cooke, Alistair. Garbo and the Nightwatchmen. London: Jonathan Cape, 1937. 352 pp.

Davy, Charles (ed.). Footnotes to the Film. London: Lovat Dickson, 1937. 346 pp.

Eisenstein, Sergei. Film Form and The Film Sense. Edited and translated by Jay Leyda. New York: Meridian Books, 1957. 561 pp.

Griffith, Richard, and Arthur Mayer. The Movies. New York: Simon and Schuster, 1957. 442 pp.

Hardy, Forsyth (ed.). Grierson on Documentary. London: Collins, 1946. 256 pp.

Harley, John Eugene. World-wide Influences of the Cinema. Los Angeles: University of Southern California Press, 1940. 320 pp.

Huntley, John. British Film Music. London: Skelton Robinson, 1947. 147 pp.

Jacobs, Lewis. The Rise of the American Film. New York: Harcourt, Brace and Company, 1939. 585 pp.

Kracauer, Siegfried. From Caligari to Hitler. Princeton, New Jersey: Princeton University Press, 1947. 361 pp.

Laclos, Michel. Le Fantastique au Cinéma. Paris: Jean-Jacques Pauvert, 1958. 197 pp.

Mallan, Lloyd. Secrets of Space Flight. Greenwich, Connecticut: Fawcett, 1956. 142 pp.

_______ (ed.). Photography Handbook. Greenwich, Connecticut: Fawcett, 1953. 144 pp.

Mantley, John. The 27th Day. Greenwich, Connecticut: Fawcett (Crest Books), 1958.

Manvell, Roger. The Animated Film. London: Sylvan Press, 1954. 63 pp.

_______. Film. Second edition. Harmondsworth, Middlesex: Penguin Books (Pelican Books), 1950. 288 pp.

_______ The Film and the Public. Harmondsworth, Middlesex: Penguin Books (Pelican Books), 1955. 352 pp.

_______ (ed.) (in collaboration with Neilson-Baxter, R. K., and Wollenberg, H. H.). The Cinema 1950. Harmondsworth, Middlesex: Penguin Books (Pelican Books), 1950. 224 pp.

_______, and R. K. Neilson-Baxter (eds.). The Cinema 1951. Harmondsworth, Middlesex: Penguin Books (Pelican Books), 1951. 224 pp.

_______, and R. K. Neilson-Baxter (eds.). The Cinema 1952. Harmondsworth, Middlesex: Penguin Books (Pelican Books), 1952. 224 pp.

Miller, Diane Disney (as told to Pete Martin). The Story of Walt Disney. New York: Dell Books, 1959. 223 pp.

Rotha, Paul. The Film Till Now. London: Jonathan Cape, 1930. 362 pp.

Rotha, Paul, and Roger Manvell. Movie Parade. Second edition. London: The Studio, 1950. 160 pp.

Scheuer, Steven H. TV Movie Almanac and Ratings, 1958 and 1959. New York: Bantam Books, 1958. 244 pp.

Sheridan, Martin. Comics and Their Creators. Boston: Ralph T. Hale and Company, 1942. 304 pp.

Slesar, Henry. Twenty Million Miles to Earth. (Amazing Stories Science Fiction Novel). New York: Ziff-Davis, 1957. 130 pp.

Smith, Robert. Riders to the Stars. (Based on the screenplay by Curt Siodmak.) New York: Ballantine Books, 1953. 166 pp.

Stuart, W. J. Forbidden Planet. (Based on the screenplay by Cyril Hume.) New York: Bantam Books, 1956. 184 pp.

Swift, Jonathan. Gulliver's Travels. New York: Ransom House (Modern Library Paperbacks), 1950. 550 pp.

Wells, H. G. Seven Famous Novels. Garden City, New York: Garden City, 1934. 860 pp.

_______. Things to Come: A Film by H. G. Wells. New York: Macmillan, 1935. 155 pp

Williamson, J. E. Twenty Years Under the Sea. New York: Hale, Cushman and Flint, 1936. 320 pp.

Wright, S. Fowler. Deluge. New York: Cosmopolitan Book Corporation, 1928. 395 pp.

B. BOOKS: PARTS OF SERIES

Aaronson, Charles S. (ed.). 1956 International Motion Picture Almanac. New York: Quigley, 1955. 902 pp.

Alicoate, Jack (ed.). The 1950 Film Daily Year Book of Motion Pictures. New York: The Film Daily, 1950. 1216 pp.

_______ The 1951 Film Daily Year Book of Motion Pictures. New York: The Film Daily, 1951. 1152 pp.

Alicoate, Jack (ed.). The 1952 Film Daily Year Book of Motion Pictures. New York: The Film Daily, 1952. 1152 pp.

________. The 1953 Film Daily Year Book of Motion Pictures. New York: The Film Daily, 1953. 1152 pp.

________. The 1954 Film Daily Year Book of Motion Pictures. New York: The Film Daily, 1954. 1280 pp.

________. The 1955 Film Daily Year Book of Motion Pictures. New York: The Film Daily, 1955. 1264 pp.

________. The 1956 Film Daily Year Book of Motion Pictures. New York: The Film Daily, 1956. 1280 pp.

________. The 1957 Film Daily Year Book of Motion Pictures. New York: The Film Daily, 1957. 1280 pp.

McCourt, A. L. (ed.). Film World 16mm Film and Industry Directory, 1949-1950. Hollywood: C. J. Ver Halen, Jr., 1949. 550 pp.

Ramsaye, Terry (ed.). 1946-47 International Motion Picture Almanac. New York: Quigley, 1946. 1024 pp.

C. PERIODICALS

Ackerman, Forrest J "Alice in Monsterland," Famous Monsters of Filmland, 1:10-23, 1958.

________. "Confessions of a Science Fiction Addict," After Hours, 1:9-13, 18-22, 1957.

________. "How Hollywood Creates a Monster," Famous Monsters of Filmland, 1:46-51, 1958.

________. "Monsters Are Badder Than Ever," Famous Monsters of Filmland, 1:8-25, 1959.

________. "The Monster Who Made a Man," Famous Monsters of Filmland, 1:26-35, 1959.

________. "Out of This World Monsters," Famous Monsters of Filmland, 1:38-45, 1958.

Ackerman, Forrest J "Scientifilm Parade," Spaceway, April, 1954, pp. 89-93.

_______, December, 1954, pp. 94-96.

_______, February, 1955, pp. 81-83.

_______, April, 1955, pp. 65-67.

_______, June, 1955, pp. 64-65, 83.

Ackerman, Forrest J "The Shape of Things To Come," Famous Monsters of Filmland, April, 1959, pp. 8-31.

Alpert, Hollis. "SRL Goes to the Movies," Saturday Review of Literature, April 21, 1951, p. 28.

_______, and Charles Beaumont. "The Horror of It All," Playboy, March, 1959, pp. 68, 74, 76, 86-88.

Beaumont, Charles. "The Science Screen," The Magazine of Fantasy and Science Fiction, September, 1955, pp. 47-51.

_______, December, 1955, pp. 67-70.

_______, March, 1956, pp. 71-74.

_______, June, 1956, pp. 75-81.

_______, December, 1957, pp. 63-65.

Berg, Louis. "Hollywood Discovers Mars," This Week, September 14, 1952, p. 9.

_______. "Reaching for the Moon," This Week, April 23, 1950, p. 18.

"Bloodstream Green," Time, October 19, 1953, p. 112.

Bowen, Elizabeth. "Things to Come: A Critical Appreciation," Sight and Sound, Spring, 1936, pp. 10-12.

Butler, Charles A. "Film Reviews," Films in Review, May, 1957, p. 222.

"Cinema," Time, October 10, 1932, p. 32.

________, April 8, 1940, p. 83.

________, August 8, 1949, p. 70.

________, December 25, 1950, p. 56.

________, May 14, 1951, p. 110.

________, January 14, 1952, p. 92.

________, April 14, 1952, p. 108.

________, February 16, 1953, pp. 104-106.

________, June 22, 1953, p. 88.

________, July 6, 1953, p. 86.

________, March 15, 1954, p. 106.

________, July 19, 1954, pp. 78-79.

________, July 11, 1955, p. 94.

________, October 8, 1956, p. 108.

"Civilization Ends—Again," Quick, October 29, 1951, p. 56.

"The Complete Story of Rodan, The Flying Monster," Monsters and Things, April, 1958, p. 36.

Connor, Edward. "Angels on the Screen," Films in Review, August-September, 1958, pp. 375-379.

Cooke, Alistair. "Films of the Quarter," Sight and Sound, Spring, 1936, pp. 24-26.

"The Current Cinema," The New Yorker, February 24, 1945, p. 55.

"Destination Moon," Life, April 24, 1950, pp. 107-110.

Dunham, Harold. "Bessie Love," Films in Review, February, 1959, pp. 86-99.

Dyer, Peter John. "New Films," Films and Filming, May, 1957, p. 28.

_______. "Some Nights of Horror," Films and Filming, July, 1958, pp. 13-15, 34-35.

_______. "Some Personal Visions," Films and Filming, November, 1958, pp. 13-15, 30-31.

Edwards, Roy. "Book Reviews," Sight and Sound, Autumn, 1958, p. 326.

_______. "Film Reviews—In Brief," Sight and Sound, Summer, 1955, p. 54.

_______. "Movie Gothick: A Tribute to James Whale," Sight and Sound, Autumn, 1957, pp. 95-98.

"Escape to the Stars," Parade, August 5, 1951, pp. 22-23.

Everson, William K. "Film Spectacles," Films in Review, November, 1954, pp. 459-471.

_______. "Horror Films," Films in Review, January, 1954, pp. 12-13.

_______. "Movies Out of Thin Air," Films in Review, April, 1955, pp. 171-180.

"Film Reviews—In Brief," Sight and Sound, Summer, 1955, p. 54.

"Flash Gordon's Trip to Mars," Look, March 15, 1938, pp. 59-61.

Folsey, George. "The Filming of Forbidden Planet." American Cinematographer, August, 1955, pp. 460-461, 482-484.

Gay, Ken. "New Films," Films and Filming, October, 1956, p. 27.

_______. "Regaining the Poetry of the Cinema," Films and Filming, December, 1956, p. 33.

Gehman, Richard. "The Hollywood Horrors," Cosmopolitan, November, 1958, pp. 38-42.

George, Manfred. "Hildegarde Neff," Films in Review, November, 1955, pp. 445-448.

"German Trade Notes," The Moving Picture World, April 1, 1916, p. 71.

Gerstein, Evelyn. "Moving Pictures," Nation, March 23, 1927, pp. 323-324.

Gerstlé, Ralph. "Film Reviews," Films in Review, January, 1955, pp. 34-35

Giesler, Rodney. "New Films," Films and Filming, July, 1956, p. 22.

Grotjahn, Dr. Martin. "Horror—Yes, It Can Do You Good," Films and Filming, November, 1958, p. 9

"A Guide to Current Films," Sight and Sound, Autumn, 1956, p. 112.

_______, Summer, 1957, p. 54.

"Half Human!" Monsters and Things, January, 1959, pp. 7-9.

Hart, Henry. "Film Reviews," Films in Review, November, 1956, pp. 463-464.

Hartung, Philip T "The Screen," Commonweal, May 14, 1954, p. 145.

_______, December 13, 1957, p 288.

Heinlein, Robert A. "Shooting Destination Moon," Astounding Science Fiction, July, 1950, pp. 6-18.

Heller, Paul. "Film Reviews," Films in Review, August-September, 1954, pp. 368-369.

Hill, Derek. "The Face of Horror," Sight and Sound, Winter, 1958-59, pp. 6-11

_______, "Film Reviews—In Brief," Sight and Sound, Spring, 1956, p. 198.

_______, "New Films," Films and Filming, August, 1955, p. 17.

Hine, Al. "Pagans and Planets," Holiday, November, 1951, pp. 24-26.

Houston, Penelope. "Red Planet Mars," Sight and Sound, October-December, 1952, p. 81.

"Huge Props to Shrink a Man," Life, May 13, 1957, p. 143.

"Jules Verne's Amazing Vision: Life in America in 2890," This Week, December 28, 1958, pp. 8-13.

Knight, Arthur. "SRL Goes to the Movies," Saturday Review of Literature, May 5, 1951, p. 26.

______. "SR Goes to the Movies," The Saturday Review, September 12, 1953, p. 47.

Laitin, Joseph. "Monsters Made to Order," Collier's, December 10, 1954, pp. 52-53.

"Letters," It, Winter, 1956, pp. 76-86.

Lobsenz, Norman M. "The Trend of S-F Movies—," Amazing Stories, January, 1959, p. 5.

Mannock, P. L. "New Films," Films and Filming, November, 1956, p. 24.

Maxwell, Hal. "Film Reviews," Films in Review, April, 1956, pp. 174-176.

Mayer, Arthur. "Hollywood: Save the Flowers," The Saturday Review, March 29, 1958, pp. 11-13, 30-32.

McCarten, John. "The Current Cinema," The New Yorker, May 12, 1951, p. 93.

"Meet Jungle Sam," Life, March 23, 1953, pp. 79-81.

Monjo, Nicolas. "Film Reviews," Films in Review, May, 1954, pp. 244-245.

"The Moon: Myths, Marvels and Man's Reach for It," Life, December 15, 1958, pp. 89-97.

Morgan, James. "Film Reviews—In Brief," Sight and Sound, Winter, 1956-57, p. 154.

Moskowitz, Sam. "Cyrano de Bergerac: Swordsman of Space," Satellite Science Fiction, March, 1959, pp. 30-36.

"Motion Picture Previews," National Parent Teacher, June, 1953, pp. 36-37.

_______, June, 1956, pp. 35-37.

_______, March, 1957, pp. 37-38.

_______, May, 1957, pp. 35-37.

"Movie of the Week," Quick, October 22, 1951, p. 59.

"Movies," Life, March 17, 1947, pp. 75-81.

"Movies," Newsweek, June 5, 1950, p. 86.

_______, May 7, 1951, p. 90.

_______, October 1, 1951, p. 90.

_______, December 1, 1952, p. 82.

_______, March 2, 1953, p. 91.

_______, January 4, 1954, p. 61.

_______, June 7, 1954, p. 56.

_______, May 14, 1956, p. 126.

_______, March 11, 1957, p. 106.

Neergaard, Ebbe. "The Rise, The Fall, and the Rise of Danish Film," Hollywood Quarterly, Spring, 1950, pp. 215-230.

"Neighbor is Nearer: Eyes of Earth Are Trained on Mars," Life, September 24, 1956, pp. 36-41.

"New Films," Films and Filming, February, 1957, p. 24.

Orna, Bernard. "New Films," Films and Filming, May, 1955, p. 18.

Pal, George. "Filming War of the Worlds," Astounding Science Fiction, October, 1953, pp. 100-111.

Peet, Creighton. "The Movies," Outlook, January 1, 1930, p. 33.

Phipps, Courtland. "Film Reviews," Films in Review, August-September, 1956, pp. 345-346.

"A Plush Parlor for Captain Nemo," Life, January 10, 1955, pp. 42-43.

"Preview," Films and Filming, February, 1956, p. 22.

"Preview of Michael Todd's Around the World in 80 Days," Films and Filming, May, 1957, pp. 20-22.

"Red's-Eye View of U. S.," Life, October 11, 1954, pp. 83-88.

Richardson, R. S. "Making Worlds Collide," Astounding Science Fiction, November, 1951, pp. 83-97.

Richie, Donald. "The Unexceptional Japanese Films," Films in Review, June-July, 1955, pp. 273-277.

"Rodan, The Flying Monster," Monsters and Things, January, 1959, pp. 40-41.

Rotha, Paul. "Films of the Quarter," Sight and Sound, Winter, 1933-34, pp. 140-144.

Sargeant, Winthrop. "Through the Interstellar Looking Glass," Life May 21, 1951, pp. 127-130 et seqq.

"Saucerman Menace," World Famous Creatures, February, 1959, pp. 14-17.

Seldes, Gilbert. "Man Ray and Metropolis," The New Republic, March 30, 1927, pp. 170-171.

Shearer, Lloyd. "The Movies' New Craze—Horror," Parade, April 20, 1958, pp. 12-15.

"Speaking of Pictures," Life, November 14, 1938, pp. 2-5.

Spears, Jack. "The Doctor on the Screen," Films in Review, November, 1955, pp. 436-444.

Springer, John. "Movie Memory Test: II," Films in Review, May, 1955, pp. 220-229.

Stimson, Thomas E., Jr. "Rocket to the Moon: No Longer a Fantastic Dream," Popular Mechanics, May, 1950, pp. 89-94.

"Tin Can Monsters," World Famous Creatures, December, 1958, pp. 28-31.

Wager, Walter. "How to Scare Up a Fast Buck," Bachelor, February, 1958, pp. 36-38, 71.

Waley, H. D. "Book Reviews," Sight and Sound, Spring, 1936, pp. 43-44.

"War of the Worlds," Collier's, October 4, 1952, pp. 50-51.

"War of the Worlds," Look, May 19, 1953, pp. 118-119.

"The War of the Worlds," Science-Fiction Plus, August, 1953, p. 67.

Wilson, N. Hope. "Film Reviews," Films in Review, March, 1954, pp. 142-143.

D. ESSAYS AND ARTICLES IN COLLECTIONS

Fabun, Don. "Science Fiction in Motion Pictures, Radio and Television," Modern Science Fiction: Its Meaning and Its Future, Reginald Bretnor, editor (New York: Coward-McCann, 1953), pp. 43-70.

Heinlein, Robert A. "Destination Moon," Three Times Infinity, Leo Margulies, editor (New York: Bantam Books, 1958), pp. 122-176.

Tors, Ivan. "Science Fiction," TV and Screen Writing, Lola G. Yoakem, editor (Berkeley and Los Angeles: University of California Press, 1958), pp. 54-58.

E. UNPUBLISHED MATERIALS

Lee, Walter W., Jr. "Science Fiction and Fantasy Films: A Preliminary Bibliography." Beverly Hills, California, 1957. 23 pp. (Rexographed.)

_______. "Science Fiction and Fantasy Film Checklist: Summer, 1958." Los Angeles, 1958. 59 + xv pp. (Mimeographed.)

Menville, Douglas. "The Science-Fiction Film: A Brief History and Criticism." An informal report written for a class in Cinema at The University of Southern California, Los Angeles, 1958. 11 pp.

Nealon, Jack. "An Historical and Critical Survey of the American Horror Film Since 1930." Unpublished Master's thesis, The University of Southern California, Los Angeles, 1953. 275 pp.

O'Brien, Willis. "Ring Around Saturn (The Beast of Hollow Mountain)." Based on an original idea by Willis O'Brien, screenplay by Paul Rader. Los Angeles, Nassour Studios, Inc., 1954. 122 pp.

Seeley, E. S., Jr. "The Sun Demon." Original screenplay by E. S. Seeley, Jr. Beverly Hills, California, Clarke-King Enterprises, 1957. 126 pp.

Tuber, Richard. "A Quantitative Analysis of Science Fiction Films, 1945-1957." An informal report written for a class in Cinema at The University of Southern California, Los Angeles, 1958. 34 pp.

F. CATALOGS AND BROCHURES

"Brandon International Film Classics Rental Catalog." New York: Brandon Films, Inc., 1957. 132 pp.

"A Catalog of the Experimental Cinema." New York: Cinema 16, 1957. 21 pp.

"Cinema 2." Hampton Bays, New York: Hampton Books, 1958. 40 pp.

"Contemporary Films." New York: Contemporary Films, Inc., 1956. 73 pp.

Edmunds, Larry. "Larry Edmunds' Bookshop: Cinema List." Los Angeles, 1958. 36 pp.

"Encyclopaedia Britannica Films Science Catalog of Audio-Visual Materials." Wilmette, Illinois: Encyclopaedia Britannica Films, 1958. 25 pp.

"Films Incorporated General Entertainment Catalog." Wilmette, Illinois: Films Incorporated, 1957. 80 pp.

"Films Incorporated Recreational 1956-1957 Catalog." Wilmette, Illinois: Films Incorporated, 1958. 80 pp.

"International Film Classics." San Francisco, California: Audio Film Classics, 1957. 34 pp.

"1945 Blue List Catalog of Selected Motion Pictures." New York: Brandon Films, Inc., 1945. 129 pp.

"La Production Cinématographique Française," January-March, 1956. Paris: UniFrance Film. 33 pp.

Rohauer, Raymond. "Coronet Film Museum Program," September, 1956-April, 1959. Los Angeles: Society of Cinema Arts.

Smith, Howard K. "Howard K. Smith Films, Inc." Los Angeles: Howard K. Smith, Inc., 1957. 74 pp.

"Twyman Films, Inc." Dayton, Ohio: Twyman Films, Inc., 1946. 116 pp.

"UniJapan Film Quarterly," July, 1958. Tokyo: Association for the Diffusion of Japanese Films Abroad, Inc. 42 pp.

"UniJapan Film Quarterly," October, 1958. Tokyo: Association for the Diffusion of Japanese Films Abroad, Inc. 42 pp.

"United World Films, Inc." (College and Institutional Edition.) New York: United World Films, Inc., 1959. 64 pp.

"University of Southern California Film Catalog." Los Angeles: Department of Cinema, The University of Southern California, 1958. 86 pp.

G. NEWSPAPERS

The Daily Trojan, October 12, 1956.

Daily Variety, September 20, 1957.

_______, October 10, 1957.

_______, October 22, 1957.

_______, October 28, 1957.

Desick, S. A. "Shrinking Man Effects Good," *Los Angeles Examiner*, March 28, 1957.

The Hollywood Reporter, November 18, 1957. (27th Anniversary Edition.)

The New York Herald Tribune, April 7, 1944.

The New York Times, January 11, 1936.

_______, March 19, 1941.

_______, April 8, 1944.

The New York World Telegram, April 7, 1944.

Scheuer, Philip K. "A Town Called Hollywood: Wail of Tortured Electrons Provides Eerie Film Score," *Los Angeles Times*, February 26, 1956.

APPENDIX

TABLE I

NUMBER OF SCIENCE FICTION FILMS PRODUCED DURING THE YEARS 1900-1950 (INCLUDING SERIALS)

Year	U.S.	Britain	France	Germany	Italy	Other
1900	0	0	1	0	0	0
1901	0	0	0	0	0	0
1902	0	0	1	0	0	0
1903	0	0	1	0	0	0
1904	0	0	1	0	0	0
1905	0	0	0	0	0	0
1906	0	0	1	0	0	0
1907	0	0	2	0	0	0
1908	1	0	1	0	0	0
1909	1	0	1	0	0	0
1910	2	0	1	0	0	0
1911	0	0	1	0	1	0
1912	0	0	0	0	0	0
1913	0	0	0	0	0	0
1914	0	0	1	0	0	0
1915	1	0	0	0	0	0
1916	4	0	1	2	0	0
1917	0	0	0	0	0	0
1918	0	0	0	0	0	2[a]
1919	0	0	0	0	0	0
1920	1	0	0	0	0	1[b]
1921	2	0	0	0	0	0
1922	2	0	0	0	0	0
1923	0	0	2	0	0	0
1924	2	0	0	0	0	0

NOTE: The superscripts refer to the following code: a—one film each produced by Denmark and Russia; b—produced by Russia (a total of four); c—produced by Bavaria; d—produced by Sweden; e—produced by Mexico. The total science fiction film output for the period from 1900 to 1950 was 119.

TABLE I, continued

Year	U.S.	Britain	France	Germany	Italy	Other
1925	2	0	0	0	0	0
1926	0	0	0	2	0	0
1927	0	0	0	0	0	0
1928	0	0	0	1	0	0
1929	1	0	0	1	0	0
1930	2	1	0	1	0	0
1931	0	0	1	1	0	0
1932	2	0	0	1	0	0
1933	7	0	0	1	0	0
1934	1	1	0	2	0	0
1935	4	1	0	0	0	1[b]
1936	3	1	0	0	0	0
1937	1	1	0	0	0	1[b]
1938	4	0	0	0	0	0
1939	1	0	1	0	0	0
1940	3	0	0	0	0	0
1941	2	0	0	0	0	1[c]
1942	0	0	0	0	0	0
1943	0	0	0	0	0	0
1944	1	1	0	0	0	0
1945	3	0	1	0	0	0
1946	6	0	0	0	0	0
1947	4	0	0	0	0	0
1948	2	0	0	0	0	0
1949	2	0	0	0	0	1[d]
1950	5	2	0	0	0	1[e]
Total	72	8	18	12	1	8

TABLE II

NUMBER OF SCIENCE FICTION FILMS
PRODUCED DURING THE YEARS 1951-1957
(INCLUDING SERIALS)

Year	U.S.	Britain	France	Germany	Italy	Other
1951	18	0	0	0	0	2[a]
1952	3	3	0	0	0	0
1953	21	3	1	2	0	0
1954	13	1	1	0	0	1[b]
1955	10	2	0	0	0	3[c]
1956	18	5	0	0	0	1[d]
1957	23	2	0	0	0	4[e]
Total	106	16	2	2	0	11

NOTE: a—One film each produced by Czechoslovakia and Russia; b—Produced by Austria; c—One each produced by Mexico, Czechoslovakia and Russia; d—Produced by Japan; e—Three films produced by Japan and one by Mexico. Total science-fiction film output from 1951 to 1957 is 137 films. These tables are based on research of the writer of this thesis in compiling films for inclusion in the chapter on the history of the science-fiction film (Chapter III).

INDEX OF FILMS

SCIENCE FICTION

An Arno Press Collection

FICTION

About, Edmond. **The Man with the Broken Ear.** 1872

Allen, Grant. **The British Barbarians:** A Hill-Top Novel. 1895

Arnold, Edwin L. **Lieut. Gullivar Jones:** His Vacation. 1905

Ash, Fenton. **A Trip to Mars.** 1909

Aubrey, Frank. **A Queen of Atlantis.** 1899

Bargone, Charles (Claude Farrere, pseud.). **Useless Hands.** [1926]

Beale, Charles Willing. **The Secret of the Earth.** 1899

Bell, Eric Temple (John Taine, pseud.). **Before the Dawn.** 1934

Benson, Robert Hugh. **Lord of the World.** 1908

Beresford, J. D. **The Hampdenshire Wonder.** 1911

Bradshaw, William R. **The Goddess of Atvatabar.** 1892

Capek, Karel. **Krakatit.** 1925

Chambers, Robert W. **The Gay Rebellion.** 1913

Colomb, P. et al. **The Great War of 189—.** 1893

Cook, William Wallace. **Adrift in the Unknown.** n.d.

Cummings, Ray. **The Man Who Mastered Time.** 1929

[DeMille, James]. **A Strange Manuscript Found in a Copper Cylinder.** 1888

Dixon, Thomas. **The Fall of a Nation:** A Sequel to the Birth of a Nation. 1916

England, George Allan. **The Golden Blight.** 1916

Fawcett, E. Douglas. **Hartmann the Anarchist.** 1893

Flammarion, Camille. **Omega:** The Last Days of the World. 1894

Grant, Robert et al. **The King's Men:** A Tale of To-Morrow. 1884

Grautoff, Ferdinand Heinrich (Parabellum, pseud.). **Banzai!** 1909

Graves, C. L. and E. V. Lucas. **The War of the Wenuses.** 1898

Greer, Tom. **A Modern Daedalus.** [1887]

Griffith, George. **A Honeymoon in Space.** 1901

Grousset, Paschal (A. Laurie, pseud.). **The Conquest of the Moon.** 1894

Haggard, H. Rider. **When the World Shook.** 1919

Hernaman-Johnson, F. **The Polyphemes.** 1906

Hyne, C. J. Cutcliffe. **Empire of the World.** [1910]

In The Future. [1875]

Jane, Fred T. **The Violet Flame.** 1899

Jefferies, Richard. **After London; Or, Wild England.** 1885

Le Queux, William. **The Great White Queen.** [1896]

London, Jack. **The Scarlet Plague.** 1915

Mitchell, John Ames. **Drowsy.** 1917

Morris, Ralph. **The Life and Astonishing Adventures of John Daniel.** 1751

Newcomb, Simon. **His Wisdom The Defender:** A Story. 1900

Paine, Albert Bigelow. **The Great White Way.** 1901

Pendray, Edward (Gawain Edwards, pseud.). **The Earth-Tube.** 1929

Reginald, R. and Douglas Menville. **Ancestral Voices:** An Anthology of Early Science Fiction. 1974

Russell, W. Clark. **The Frozen Pirate.** 2 vols. in 1. 1887

Shiel, M. P. **The Lord of the Sea.** 1901

Symmes, John Cleaves (Captain Adam Seaborn, pseud.). **Symzonia.** 1820

Train, Arthur and Robert W. Wood. **The Man Who Rocked the Earth.** 1915

Waterloo, Stanley. **The Story of Ab:** A Tale of the Time of the Cave Man. 1903

White, Stewart E. and Samuel H. Adams. **The Mystery.** 1907

Wicks, Mark. **To Mars Via the Moon.** 1911

Wright, Sydney Fowler. **Deluge: A Romance** *and* **Dawn.** 2 vols. in 1. 1928/1929

SCIENCE FICTION

NON-FICTION:
Including Bibliographies,
Checklists and Literary Criticism

Aldiss, Brian and Harry Harrison. **SF Horizons.** 2 vols. in 1. 1964/1965

Amis, Kingsley. **New Maps of Hell.** 1960

Barnes, Myra. **Linguistics and Languages in Science Fiction-Fantasy.** 1974

Cockcroft, T. G. L. **Index to the Weird Fiction Magazines.** 2 vols. in 1 1962/1964

Cole, W. R. **A Checklist of Science-Fiction Anthologies.** 1964

Crawford, Joseph H. et al. **"333": A Bibliography of the Science-Fantasy Novel.** 1953

Day, Bradford M. **The Checklist of Fantastic Literature in Paperbound Books.** 1965

Day, Bradford M. **The Supplemental Checklist of Fantastic Literature.** 1963

Gove, Philip Babcock. **The Imaginary Voyage in Prose Fiction.** 1941

Green, Roger Lancelyn. **Into Other Worlds:** Space-Flight in Fiction, From Lucian to Lewis. 1958

Menville, Douglas. **A Historical and Critical Survey of the Science Fiction Film.** 1974

Reginald, R. **Contemporary Science Fiction Authors,** First Edition. 1970

Samuelson, David. **Visions of Tomorrow:** Six Journeys from Outer to Inner Space. 1974